Showers

Editor: **Ruth Benedict**
Layout and Design: **Jan Kumbier**
Photography: **Mike Huibregtse**
Illustrations: **Jan Kumbier, Peggy Bjorkman**
Production: **Jan Kumbier, Tom Hunt,**
Peggy Bjorkman, Sally Radtke, Sue Kinsey

ISBN: 0-89821-030-5
Library of Congress Catalog Card Number: 79-65360

The Diary of an Incurable Shower Giver...

TO INTRODUCE this book, we asked Carol Wolf, a farm wife from Union Grove, Wis. to share some of her thoughts on the joy of giving baby and bridal showers. She's a veteran party and shower giver from way back, with plenty of experience (and happy memories!) to share—Ruth Benedict, Editor.

JUST LET the word "shower" cross my mind and a special part of me shifts into gear.

What kind of shower to have? I've kept files on the parties and showers my family has attended for the past 36 years—as long as we've been married. I've kept records of what games we've played, what food was served, who was there, the door prizes...and then I just go back and change the games and food and have another party.

And who will come? I always put a *hint* in my party invitations so people have some idea of what to expect. And for people like me who like to "think up" different showers and parties, there's hardly ever a negative RSVP. This proves to me—*people love fun.*

What's the secret? Change games you've played before, dream up interesting decorations and refreshments and make the shower *YOU*. You can't fail. In fact, most folks will laugh right along with you if something doesn't go just right.

We really love people, fun and the sound of laughter. There is so little laughter in this troubled world we live in. After a party, it's easier to face all the problems of life again.

Even the thank-you notes after you have a great shower can be fun. Once, after we had a "backwards" shower, one guest wrote a thank-you note—all backwards. We had to read it in a mirror. And since she had addressed it backwards too, it had gone back to the Milwaukee post office for someone to figure it out. But we eventually got it!

Some people feel it's a waste of time to figure out games and party plans, but I think it's so worthwhile. The happy times we've had will always be remembered. And many of the showers we've had have gotten some young couple off to a better start, or made a better nest for their new wee one.

Our daughters Peggy and Beth used to beg to stay up during party evenings at our house—going to bed was so dull! Today, they're married, and often write or call home to ask how to play a certain game or how to get a certain type of party off the ground.

I'm so glad they are passing it on. I hope you enjoy this book!

"A merry heart doth good like medicine." Proverbs 17:22

Crochet and Knit Abbreviations

ch—chain	rnd—round	sl st—slip stitch	ss—stockinette stitch
dc—double crochet	sc—single crochet	st(s)—stitch(es)	oz—ounce
hdc—half double crochet	tr—triple crochet	k—knit	beg—begin, beginning
lp—loop	sk—skip	p—purl	inc—increase
rep—repeat	sp—space	yo—yarn over	tog—together

Contents

For The Bride...

Gift Ideas 36

Shower-Perfect Recipes 48

For The Baby . . .

Invitations & Wedding Announcements

Design Your Own Invitations

Personalize your wedding day with your own announcement (or shower invitation) creations!

By Marjorie Rooney, Buffalo, Minnesota

MOST BRIDES and bridegrooms today are choosing and composing certain parts of their wedding ceremonies, and their own personalized wedding announcements.

If you have an upcoming wedding in your family and would love to produce your own announcements (but are afraid to tackle the challenge), it is easier than you think.

When our son Tim and his fiance, Britt Inger Blegen, planned their wedding to take place in Nor-way, they asked me to design their announcements. Since all of her relatives still resided in Norway, she wrote the announcement in Norwegian. I was provided with a snapshot of the church, Kolbu Kirke, from which I penned the drawing on the invitation shown on the opposite page.

The wording of the announcement follows the usual format, except that space is left in the center to fill in each recipient's name after the announcements are printed by a printing shop.

Print shops provide paper and envelopes in a variety of colors. You can draw out the entire design in india ink. We ordered special parchment paper in a beautiful soft, off-white, with matching envelopes in announcement size.

Keep in mind the folding process when you lay out your front design, and inside announcement.

Paper Flower Invitations

(See opposite page)

By Beth Tobler, Appleton, Wisconsin

THESE BRIGHT, cheerful little invitations can be made easily and with little expense. Cut circles with a paper punch, using colorful construction paper.

Remove the punched paper holes from the paper punch. Shape these little circles into flower shapes, and glue neatly onto the invitations. Paint on the stems and bow.

Write your message inside. You now have bright, cheerful shower invitations that have the personal, handmade touch.

Hope Chest Invitation

By Mrs. Rodney Voelker, Brownsdale, Minnesota

IF YOU'RE planning to have some sort of theme shower which would yield gifts appropriate for a hope chest, one cute way to carry the theme in your invitations is to write the shower information inside a pretty piece of note paper, and then fold the top and bottom until they overlap somewhere in the middle of the sheet. (See Fig. 2.)

Attach a circular self-adhesive sticker (the kind you get in fold-a-letters) and draw a keyhole shape on it. Then write "Let's fill (bride's name) Hope Chest" on the front.

Heart Invitations

By Mrs. Elroy Jensen, Canby, Minnesota

CUT OUT a pretty heart from pastel or red construction paper. Cut lace from a paper doily and paste it to the back heart around the edges as shown.

Cut rings from gold or silver foil and tie them together (gently) with a tiny ribbon. Glue the ribbon and rings to the center of the pillow to look just like a little ring bearer's pillow. Print the necessary information inside. (See Fig. 3.)

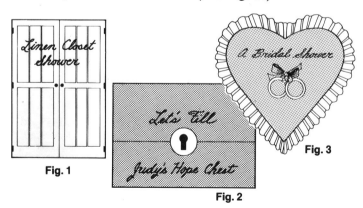

Fig. 1

Fig. 2

Fig. 3

A Linen Shower

By Mrs. Rodney Voelker, Brownsdale, Minnesota

A LINEN shower usually includes gifts such as sheets, pillowcases, towels, facecloths, tablecloths, napkins and similar articles. (See Fig. 1.)

The invitations may be written on a piece of paper in the form of a linen closet with the two sides folded in to the center to form the doors.

"Theme" Showers

Sewing Box Shower

If the bride-to-be hopes to become more of a seamstress, this is the perfect gift.

By Barbara Stock, Wilmette, Illinois

PROVIDE A sewing box—empty and as large as possible—and "assign" the fillings to your guests.

On each invitation, specify a gift: A hemmer, a tape measure, thimbles, patches, a variety of seam bindings, special fabrics, measuring tape, pinking shears, etc.

Ask younger guests short on cash to bring several shades of red, blue, green, brown or black thread. Suggest that the flower girl offer a pincushion with pins and needles to indicate her excitement. A note attached could read: "I'm on pins and needles. Will your wedding day ever come?"

Encourage those who wish to buy more expensive gifts to think of gift certificates, patterns, fabric, sewing lessons, a machine overhaul, or even a new sewing machine as presents. Have the mother of the bride present a selection of scissors to cut the wrapping cord.

A Basket Shower

By Mrs. Eugene Placek, Western, Nebraska

SEND INVITATIONS with this little verse:
"A tisket, a tasket,
Let's fill the bride a 'basket'.
See how clever you can be
Filling a basket for (bride's name).
This happy task you can share,
With one, with three or perhaps a pair,
The 'basket' we would like you to fill,
To give the bride an added thrill is
(Type of basket)   .
    Your partner(s) in this task is/are:"
(List names, telephone numbers)
    "Use either a basket, or box or wastebasket.
    There's no real need to wrap as we'll simply line up the 'baskets' and hand them to
    (bride's name) and let her show everyone the contents."

Here are basket-suggestions you could list for your guests: *Beverage,* filled with all kinds of juices, drink mixes; *Bathroom,* use a wastebasket, filled with brushes, soaps, powders; *Cleaning,* filled with cleaning items; *Paper,* with towels, stationery, toilet paper; *Brush,* filled with all kinds of brushes; *Spice,* perhaps in an attractive bread basket—plenty of nice spices; *Bottle,* with catsup, mustard, other condiments, colognes; *Grocery*—let the bride's mother or grandmother get this one; *Green Thumb,* in a bushel basket, filled with seeds, little plants, cuttings, books, fertilizer; *Glassware*—nice glasses; *Arts & Crafts,* a pillow kit, needlepoint and knitting items, instruction books; *Kitchen Gadgets,* openers, potato mashers; *Fruit and Vegetable,* home-canned produce with attractive labels, jellies; *Supper,* with Hamburger Helper, little packages of rice, ready-to-

serve or starter meals; and as many other types of baskets as you can think of.

You'll be surprised to see how few duplications there are, and the new bride gets so many terrific things to use in her new home!

At the shower, line up the baskets behind the table (with tissue paper over each) where the bride sits, and let her one by one, unwrap them.

Decorate with baskets of flowers, cupcakes served on basket-like trays, or decorate the cupcakes like baskets with flowers using the icing and pipe cleaner handles.

Pantry-Stocking Shower

By Evelyn Tuller, Elwood, Kansas

EACH GUEST should bring one paper bag of groceries. The possibilities are endless! An economical Styrofoam picnic cooler could be filled with disposable plates, cups, napkins; a garbage pail or scrub bucket filled with cleaning supplies. Toilet paper, paper tissues or towels are all items which mount up as expenses for the first-stocking of a household, but are minimal when added to an individual's weekly grocery sack.

Snack foods, home-canned goods or frozen homemade goods are also appreciated. Take the time to cut out a supply of cents-off coupons from magazines and newspapers. It will help cut down on the couple's first few trips to the grocery store.

Another idea is to bring a bag of supplies for a medicine cabinet and a household first aid box. Both are bound to come in handy at some point.

Long Distance Shower

If you'd like to honor a bride living far away, there are plenty of ways to do something special for her.

By Loula Bloomfield, Elwood, Kansas

PACK A shower box so that when your guest of honor opens it, the "shower" will unfold in logical and fun steps. (Pack the last thing you want the bride to open at the bottom of the box. Place dividing layers of tissue paper.)

At the top of the box, attach a note reading "If you were here, we'd have a shower, and at the shower we'd play some games. And if you were here and we had a shower and played some games you would get the prize—here is your prize." Have a gift there for her to open. Repeat the verse again, and have another prize. Repeat it once more and have a third.

On another card, write: "If you were here we'd have a shower and when we had the shower we'd all bring gifts—so open your gifts." Place all the gifts under this card.

For refreshment time, write a card "If you were here etc...we'd have refreshments. So here are the napkins and plates" and include shower-type napkins and plates.

Next write "If you were here etc...we would have a cake—so here's a cake." Enclose a cake mix and frosting inside a covered loaf cake pan.

If possible, have the bride or bridegroom's parents personally deliver the package to the new couple's home—or, if mailing the box (or boxes), simply number them so she'll open them in the right order.

Bathrobe Brunch Shower

By Marge Wenzel, Kent, Illinois

Materials:
scraps of print quilting fabric
scraps of felt, rickrack, other trims
old photographs (or magazine cutouts)
white paper
glue

CUT OUT a robe in the quilted fabric (see pattern on page 97), making one for each guest you intend to invite. Cut an "inner" robe by using the pattern over paper folded in half. (Be sure to line one side of the "robe" near the paper fold so you can leave a hinge of paper at the wrist).

Cut out a head from a photograph or magazine page and glue to wrong side of the quilting. Glue the paper robe on the back of the quilting. Trim the front of the robe, write your message inside, and tie a rickrack belt around the entire invitation.

A suggested "message"—"Saturday morning, Jan. 31, 9 to 12. We're having a Bridal Shower Breakfast in honor of Marcia. 'Cover Charge': Any item off your pantry shelf to help fill a grocery bag for her, and your favorite recipe on the card enclosed.

"Attire: To add to the gaiety of the occasion, please come dressed in your lounging pajamas, nightie, housecoat or robe.

"We asked Marcia what her favorite colors were and she said orange, yellow and green. Join us for lots of fun. RSVP."

A Dough Pin Party Shower

This is a good shower for a bride-to-be who's already had a number of showers.

By Michelle Talber, Vandalia, Missouri

THE MONEY from a "Dough Pin" shower will be greatly appreciated when the new couple sets up their new household.

Send out invitations with wording similar to this:

"As the bride-to-be has most everything she needs, we are going to make a 'Dough Pin' and present it to her. If you wish to contribute money for it, you may do so on arriving.

"We also plan to have a recipe exchange, so please copy your favorite recipe and bring one of the ingredients that goes into it for the bride-to-be. Also, bring plenty of extra recipe cards for yourself. We're sure you will want to copy the other guests' favorites. Hope to see you there."

On the day of the shower, have a guest book set up and ask your guests to sign it. Also have them sign a group card, and affix their "dough" to a rolling pin, which you provide. For a centerpiece, bake a loaf of bread, dry it out in the oven, and trim it with a pretty calico ribbon.

Play games for a while. After the games, each guest should one at a time give the bride her recipe and ingredient. As they give the recipe, have them tell a little bit about it, why their family likes it, etc.

While you prepare the refreshments, encourage your guests to exchange their recipes and chat.

To go along with the "dough" theme, make your refreshments of dough foods—a large danish tea ring, cinnamon twists, sweet rolls—and serve coffee, tea, punch and homemade mints.

After the refreshments, present the "Dough Pin" to the bride-to-be with a card signed by all those present. The card should read "Please remove dough before using this on pie crusts or husband!"

Ice Cream Bridal Shower

Center your shower around an ice cream theme— naturally the perfect gift for the new couple is an ice cream freezer.

By Carla Reed, Henry, Illinois

FLAVOR SCRAMBLE

MAKE A list of scrambled ice cream flavors and give your guests a few minutes to work them out. Example: butter pecan (tubtre ancpe), banana marshmallow (abnaan larmmwasolh), etc.

ICE CREAM BINGO

Make up ice cream related words on bingo cards, and when playing the game, read them aloud to your guests. (Use words like salt, sugar, Sealtest, Howard Johnson, parlor, calories, milk, cream, licking the spoon, etc.). When someone has a full card or a completed row, she should call out "Ice Cream" (instead of Bingo) and she wins. Prizes should be ice cream toppings like fudge sauce, marshmallows, a box of strawberries, etc.

REFRESHMENTS

For refreshments, serve vanilla ice cream (even better if homemade!) with all kinds of toppings for each guest to make a sundae. Serve cookies, coffee and tea.

RECIPES

Collect ice cream recipes from your guests (through the shower invitations) and present the bride with an envelope of recipes after she has opened her gifts.

Make a Money Tree

SPRAY PAINT a tree branch white, and cover with attractively-folded currency. Attach (or read) the following verse:

Money grows on trees, they say;
So proof of it has come your way.
Now, make a wish for something new
And Lo! behold it will come true.
Remove the greenbacks with utmost care
And splurge on something you can wear.
Or, perhaps it's something else you want.
We wish you luck, as you go and hunt.

Recipe Shower "Recipes"

There are plenty of different twists to get imaginations going for each and every recipe shower.

Recipe Shower Ingredients

By Estelle Salata, Hamilton, Ontario

"The recipe for a kitchen shower is easy to follow. Plan carefully. Collect the proper ingredients. Add a dash of creative ingenuity and mix together the bride, her friends, gifts, decorations and good party food. Bake in a warm, happy atmosphere. The result is a bride with cherished memories that will last forever."

Recipe Card Extras

By Mrs. Francis Snow, Mill Run, Pennsylvania

CARRY OUT your "recipe" shower theme by making a small flower arrangement inside a recipe box, and use as a centerpiece. The favors could be plastic forks, stuck handle side down in a small container of plaster of paris. The fork tines could hold a guest's recipe, to be collected later for the bride.

Read Out!

By Mrs. Randa Nill, Kulm, North Dakota

HAVE THE bride read aloud the names of the recipes she receives. What a conversation starter!

Special Serving Gift

By Norma Danielson, Cheney, Washington

ONE NICE thing for the bride is a sterling pie or cake serving knife. This can be bought with donations from the other guests, and is a nice "topper" for a recipe shower. If engraved with the wedding date or shower date, it is even more special.

Pantry Stock

ASK the guests to bring along (gift-wrapped) the key ingredient in the recipe they'll be sharing. This is a nice pantry-starter for the bride.
Entries too numerous to mention.

Cooking Bonanza

By Charlotte Roach, Faucett, Missouri

INSTEAD OF bringing the key ingredient in their recipe, each guest could bring along the key cooking utensil used for it—or a few smaller utensils used in preparation of that dish. This is an excellent way for the bride to acquire lots of good recipes and kitchen equipment at the same time.

Recipe Card Invitations

EVERY shower starts with the invitations to the guests. Send them written on recipe cards, and send extras. Ask the guests to bring along anywhere from 1-5 of their favorite recipes for the bride-to-be. *—Entries too numerous to mention.*

Friendship Tea

By Jo Wenzel, Kent, Illinois

WHEN YOU ask your new friend to put on the tea kettle and share a cup of tea with you, together you can brighten up the task of settling into a new home and neighborhood.

For the tea, use an instant coffee jar. Apply a circle of calico fabric on the lid. Decorate the sides with fabric or magazine cutouts.

Apply both the fabric and print with glue. When both pieces of fabric and paint dry, apply a coat of clear acrylic to make the covering waterproof.

Friendship Tea
  1 cup instant orange drink mix
2/3 cup instant tea
1/2 cup sugar
  1 package dry lemonade mix
1/2 teaspoon cinnamon
1/4 teaspoon cloves

Mix ingredients well. Store in tightly sealed jar. To use, add 2 teaspoons or more to a cup of hot water. Optional: Add part of a package of powdered "punch" mix to the above.

Housewarming Shower

This is a nice way to say "welcome" to new friends.

By Jean Lyon, Cedar Rapids, Iowa

MAKE IT a couples' affair, a weekend brunch or any evening potluck picnic or barbecue party. Guests could bring their own steaks and those in charge could provide steaks for the new neighbors.

If the house is new the guests could go with paint scrapers and other equipment for cleaning windows. If it's autumn the men could rake up the leaves while the wives work inside. Have a bonfire, a sing-a-long and story telling later to help everyone become better acquainted.

Gifts could range from the ridiculous to the exquisite, and would bring laughter and be an ice breaker. If each couple took a white elephant gift, such as a sack of old neck ties, off-brand lotions, out-of-date and hardened cleaning powders, unmatched glasses and other questionable items, opening the gifts after dinner would keep the conversation going and would make the newcomers feel better acquainted and part of the group.

Shower Smorgasbord

By Mrs. Rodney Voelker, Brownsdale, Minnesota

SPECIFY ON your invitations the type of food you'd like that guest to prepare for the shower. For this you must plan out a menu ahead of time, and reserve the meat or main courses dishes for yourself.

Foods your guests could bring would be salads, vegetables, casseroles, hot rolls, homemade pickles, punch or desserts—all of course, with the recipe for the dish attached to give to the bride-to-be.

Recipe Collectors

PROVIDE a pretty recipe box for the bride, and as the guests arrive, collect their cards and place them in the box. Or, have each attach recipe cards to her gift.   *—Entries too numerous to mention.*

Bread Shower

By Carol Wolf, Union Grove, Wisconsin

MAKE A centerpiece, using a shellacked loaf of bread. Give smaller loaves as prizes—they're beautiful for years!

Make each guest a favor, using a 3 x 4-inch piece of paneling. Glue on a small biscuit, and a grain weed. Shellac. Attach a tiny straw flower, and attach a "peel off" holder on the back. The guests can take them home and hang them on their kitchen wall—very attractive!

After all the gifts have been given out, give (or promise) the bride-to-be a loaf of bread for her first breakfast!

Tupperware Bridal Shower

By Anna Mary Yoder, Middlebury, Indiana

HOST A Tupperware bridal shower party, collecting money from each guest for the bride-to-be.

At the end of the demonstration, give the guest of honor the total amount collected and ask her to choose Tupperware pieces that equal the amount of cash collected.

Record Her Comments

By Mrs. Elroy Jensen, Canby, Minnesota

PLACE A small tape recorder somewhere near the guest of honor. Tape her comments while she's opening the gifts, and play back a couple of excerpts later. Lots of fun!

Bridal Shower Place Mats

By Mildred Grenier, St. Joseph, Missouri

FOR EACH place at the table, cut a large heart from red construction paper. Dip a cotton-tipped swab in household bleach and write each guest's name at the bottom of the heart.

Or, make reusable place mats for your bridal shower by cutting a strip of waxed paper the size you want your place mat to be. In each corner and in the center, place brightly-colored cutouts of hearts, rings, cupids, wedding cake, candles, gifts, a bride, etc. Place another strip of waxed paper the same size over the first one. Cover with brown paper. Press with a warm iron. The mats may be wiped off and used again and again.

Favors, Place Cards & Centerpieces

Wedding Rice

Rice is thrown on the bride and bridegroom on their wedding day to ensure fruitfulness and abundance. Rice is considered a symbol of best wishes and good luck.

Scented Tinted Rice

COLORED RICE has a special meaning for wedding days—blue for fidelity, yellow for cheer, and red for passion. You can make these, or other colors to compliment the wedding's color scheme.

Materials:
1 cup water
1/2 to 1 teaspoon food coloring
dash of perfume or cologne
2-1/3 cups (1 pound) uncooked rice (be sure to use regular milled white rice for pastel shades, and parboiled rice for darker shades. Pre-cooked rice not recommended.)

Mix water with food coloring in a 1-quart glass or metal bowl. Stir in perfume. (Cologne or perfume may also be dashed or sprayed on the rice after it has been dried.)

Then add rice. Let stand about 5 minutes, or until rice is a shade darker than desired color. (Color will lighten as rice dries.)

Drain, reserving colored water for next batch. Spread rice in the bottom of a jelly roll pan or cookie sheet. Place in preheated 250° oven for 15 minutes, stirring occasionally during drying. Remove from oven and pour rice onto paper towels. Let stand, uncovered, overnight to allow to dry thoroughly. Makes 36 tablespoons tinted rice, or enough for 18-36 rice souvenir bags (shown below). Repeat this process for each new color desired.

Rice Souvenir Bags

Materials:
scented, tinted rice
sheer, close-weave fabric (tulle, dotted swiss, etc.)
ribbon or cord

FIRST, COLOR and thoroughly dry and cool the rice. Cut fabric into 5-inch squares and cut ribbon into 4-inch lengths. Place 1 tablespoon of rice in the center of each fabric square. Bring the 4 corners of fabric together and tie with ribbon.

For larger bags, use 6-inch squares of fabric, 2 tablespoons of rice and 6-inch lengths of ribbon.

Rice Nosegay

USE THESE in combination with The Tree of Life (shown below) or in place of it.

Cut 5-inch squares from clear plastic refrigerator wrap. In each square place 2 teaspoons of tinted-scented rice.

Pull all four corners together and twist to form a small bag. In the center of a white or colored round 6-inch doily, punch one hole for each rice bag. Pull the twisted corners of each bag through a hole in the doily. Then pull all ends of the bags together and secure with a rubber band.

Use 1/8-inch or 1/4-inch wide white or colored ribbon to make a bow to cover the rubber band. Leave ends of the ribbon as long as you desire.

The Tree of Life

USE A NATURAL tree limb about 2-3 feet high with small branches (or use a plastic tree). Paint it white and secure it in a thick block or circle of Styrofoam so it will stand alone.

Cover the Styrofoam with white ribbon. Tie the small colorful Rice Souvenir Bags on the branches. Place in center of table and surround with additional bags of tinted rice.

Honeymoon Sachets

THE SMALL bags of scented rice may be used as sachets. Their fragrance endures long past the honeymoon.

—These five rice ideas come from The Rice Council of America

Rice for Shower Guests

By Marge Wenzel, Kent, Illinois

MAKE A basket of rice bags—and your shower guests will be able to bring them to the wedding to toss at the new couple.

Using colored net, tie up 1/4 to 1/2 cup of rice in a small net square. Tie with a satin ribbon, and attach a slip of paper with this verse on it:

"A shower of rice the day they are wed
Will bring good luck it has been said.
So take this rice and put it away
For_____and_____wedding day!"
   (bride's name)   (bridegroom's name)

Thimble-Sized Wedding Bells

Make these thimble-sized bells for a bridal centerpiece.

Crocheted Bells

By Eva Segar, Hamilton, Missouri

(See crochet abbreviations on page 2.)

Materials:
size 30 white crochet thread
size 12 crochet hook
piece of round or oval Styrofoam—about
  6-8 inches in diameter
chenille wires in the wedding colors
small dried flowers
lace or nylon net, ribbon, trim, etc. (If the
  bride's gown is handmade, a scrap from
  that makes the centerpiece personal.)
1 tablespoon sugar
1 tablespoon hot water

18 INCHES from end of crochet thread, ch 4; sl st in 1st st making circle.
  1st row: 7 sc into circle.
  2nd row: 2 sc into next 7 sc.
  Next rows: 1 sc into each sc until bell is 3/4 inch.
  Last row: 2 sc into next 14 sc; sl st into next sc; cut thread 1/4 inch. Ch 6 of the 18 inches you saved at beg; sl st to top of bell. This forms handle. Turn bell wrong side out, pull thread through hold and ch 8, sc 4 times in 6th ch for clapper; sl st to 5th ch. Cut thread 1/4 inch; turn bell right side out.
  Mix water and sugar, soak bell, shape, press loose cut ends of thread against work. It will keep its shape when dried. Dry on hard surface.
  To make bell centerpiece: Place net or lace over the Styrofoam. Wrap lace or trim around it to cover raw edges. Secure with glue or straight pins.

Cut off excess lace or net. Thread pipe cleaners through handles of two bells. Form into the shape of a heart and push into Styrofoam. Arrange dried flowers, add a bow or other finishing touches.

Knit Bells

(See knitting abbreviations on page 2.)

Materials:
size 30 white crochet thread
4 round toothpicks
size 12 crochet hook

CAST ON 2 sts on each of 3 toothpicks.
  1st row: K circular.
  2nd row: Inc 1 st in each st (12 sts in all).
  Next rows: K circular for 3/4 inch.
  Last row: Inc. 1 st in each of next 12 sts (24 sts in all). Bind off.
  Finish as for crocheted bells.

Bell Tree Centerpiece

By Mrs. Frank DeHaas, Greencreek, Idaho

Materials:

a small tree branch	narrow satin ribbon
plaster of paris	mints
thread	paper nut cups
plastic filigree bells	white spray paint
15-inch wide strip of net, plus scraps	

SPRAY A small branch with white spray paint and place it in a can of plaster of paris. Cover the can with a strip of net to decorate outside.

Put a gathering thread about 2 inches from the end. Pull up the thread tightly around the bottom of the branch to cover the can.

Decorate the branch with bells tied on with satin ribbon. (Use the bride's colors!) Make nut cups and set them around the centerpiece for added decoration. Fill any extra bells with mints, and cover with net. (Be sure to cut the net squares large enough so they can be pulled up tightly and tied at the tip with a satin ribbon.)

Happy Marriage Pattern

A little collection of good advice!

By Evelyn Carson Tuller, Elwood, Kansas

ASK YOUR guests to bring a favorite recipe. Make an envelope the same size as a dress pattern envelope and draw a picture of a bride in her wedding gown on the front. On the top, write "Pattern for a Happy Marriage", and write the date of the shower across the bottom.

Place the recipe cards and plenty of extra "blanks" inside the envelope. On the back, write the following information as the "pattern guide:"

Material Required
Love, patience and understanding,
Humor, faithfulness and a touch of wit.

Notions Needed
Wisdom of Solomon, patience of Job,
A thread of humor and a zipper for your lip.

Proper Measurements
Is your understanding wide enough?
Your patience long enough?
Your love? We know it's deep enough.

Planning the Layout
Don't worry about who is head of the household. Pin your hopes on cooperation.

Seam Allowance
Give a little. Losing the battle can win love as well as wars.

Cutting Instructions
Cutting words can ruin this pattern.

Ruffling
Ruffling feathers, as well as "ruffled ones", are definitely not called for.

Finishing Details
Flattery will get you far in sewing up a happy marriage.

Washcloth Nosegay

By Marie Hellinger, Shelby, Montana

Materials:
10 lightweight washcloths (2 green ones for leaves and stems; the rest in pastel colors)
 1 9-inch firm cardboard circle
 1 white paper plate
round lace paper doilies or lace fabric cut at least 1 inch larger than cardboard circle
pins, thread, glue, string
several artificial flowers
 2 2-foot lengths of narrow ribbon in coordinating colors

COVER CARDBOARD circle with the paper doilies or fabric, turn under and glue. Glue paper plate to the back to cover glued edges. When dry, cut a 1-inch hole in the center. Place the two green washcloths (unfolded) on the circle as shown.

Using your finger, poke the washcloths (Fig. 1) through the hole until a "stem" is made, about 3 inches long. Stitch the stem to make a finished edge.

To make each washcloth flower, open the washcloth. Fold in two opposite corners until they overlap as shown (Fig. 2) and fold again along longest middle line (Fig. 3).

Start rolling loosely from one end, and tie a string about 1/4 of the way up from the bottom to hold (Fig. 4). Pin securely or stitch loose edge.

Arrange the "flowers" on the lace circle, and stitch in place. Pin or tack remaining corners of the green washcloths in place to resemble leaves. Fill in open areas with artificial flowers or leaves and small ribbon bows. Tie the streamers of ribbon to the stem.

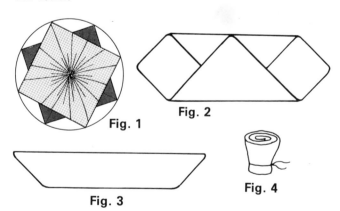

Fig. 1   Fig. 2

Fig. 3   Fig. 4

Teatime Centerpiece

By Estelle Salata, Hamilton, Ontario

ARRANGE a nice cup and saucer, a yellow-enameled coffee or teapot (or copper teakettle or china pitcher and basin) brimming with garden flowers in the center of the table. As hostess, this could be your gift to the bride-to-be.

Archway Centerpiece

Here's the perfect way to decorate a fancy shower table with a pretty touch.

Materials:
4 37 x 1/2-inch strips of pliable wood
small nails
glue
4 x 12-inch board for base
popsicle sticks
white spray paint
wire
green plastic leaves
artificial flowers
several "fashion" dolls
2 1/2 x 10-inch sticks

BEND each of the 37-inch sticks into the shape of an arch. Nail or glue them to the sides of the 4- x 12-inch board, spacing evenly. Glue popsicle sticks horizontally over the entire arch, leaving about ½-inch space between each stick. Allow to dry.

Spray paint the entire arch and base white. When dry, wire on leaves and flowers. Construct the picket fence around the base, by cutting popsicle sticks in half and gluing them onto 2½- x 10-inch sticks.

Dress 3 Barbie (or other small fashion) dolls, one in a bridal gown, and the others in whatever colors the wedding party may be using. Place them on the base, the bride under the archway and the bridesmaids behind the picket fences.

Ring Box Favor

By Esther Fahning, Wells, Minnesota

CUT TWO small hearts from Styrofoam, and hinge together like a ring box with a pipe cleaner cut in half. Glue scraps of knit fabric cut to size around the edges of each heart. Glue a flower applique on top. Inside, place two tiny curtain rings, painted gold or silver.

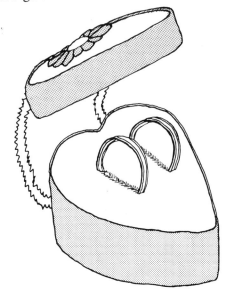

Baked Centerpiece?

By Estelle Salata, Hamilton, Ontario

BAKE AN angel food cake and put an eggcup or other small container of water in the center. Fill with pansies or other miniature flowers.

Or, scoop out a large hole in the center of a loaf of bread. Place a small glass or container of water into the hole. Fill with a bouquet of miniature flowers.

Another way to make a "baked" centerpiece is to insert the legs of a teen doll into a round cake which has been decorated with white and pink icing to resemble a full skirt.

Silver Bell Favor

By Mildred Grenier, St. Joseph, Missouri

MOLD aluminum foil over the small egg-cup sections cut from a cardboard or plastic egg carton. Tie a small knot in the end of a strip of narrow white ribbon, and run the ribbon through a hole in the top of the bell; tie several bells together with a pretty bow at the top. Silver ribbon can be used, in place of the white. Use on cakes, packages or as favors.

Wedding Rings Place Cards

These place cards are so pretty everyone will want to take them home as a special keepsake!

By Mrs. LaVerne Majerus, Brownsdale, Minnesota

MAKE A folded card from stiff paper 3½ inches square. Draw a border around, if you'd like, using colored ink. Punch two holes in the upper left hand corner.

Dip two curtain rings in gold paint. When dry, tie to card with narrow satin ribbon. Insert a couple of small dried flowers.

Apron Nametags

By Carol Wolf, Union Grove, Wisconsin

CUT OUT tiny gingham aprons, and sew on tiny ties. Give one to each guest, as a name tag. Or, use them as favors.

At gift time, give the bride-to-be an apron for her new home.

Coffee Scoop Favor

By Mrs. Clifford Johnson, Owatonna, Minnesota

FILL COLORED plastic coffee measuring scoops with candy or nuts. Place ribbon and tiny artificial flowers on the handle. Print the guest's name on the outside of the scoop (Fig. 1).

Wheelbarrow Nut Cup

By Mrs. Clifford Johnson, Owatonna, Minnesota

PUT A plastic soda straw through a lifesaver, and then put the straw through holes punched in a paper nut cup, as shown. Fill the tiny wheelbarrow with nuts or candy (Fig. 2).

Fern Place Cards

By Mrs. Clifford Johnson, Owatonna, Minnesota

WELL before the shower, pick a few fronds of fern and dry them between layers of paper for several days. Arrange them on the bottom half of the sticky side of a rectangle of adhesive-backed paper. Write one guest's name alongside and fold into a place card. Cover the entire rectangle with plastic wrap (Fig. 3).

Pretty Napkin Holders

By Mrs. Clifford Johnson, Owatonna, Minnesota

CUT a construction paper heart 3 or 4 inches wide. Glue on a lace edging cut from a paper doily.

About 3/4 inch from each edge (as shown), cut a slit. Insert a long paper arrow cutout. Roll a paper napkin and insert between the arrow and back of heart. Add name (Fig. 4).

Fig. 3

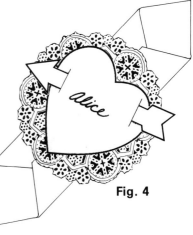

Fig. 4

Fig. 1

Fig. 2

Games

Bride Bingo

Bingo is a perfect ice-breaker for a shower...and with a bridal (or baby) twist.

BEFORE THE shower, make up as many player cards as you expect you'll need—either on large sheets of paper or 5- x 7-inch index cards. Write in B-R-I-D-E across the top, and draw in spaces below the letters B-R-I-D-E, as shown opposite.

Fill in the spaces differently on each card, using any number of the following words: Wedding, honeymoon, mother-in-law, bridesmaid, minister, bridegroom, bouquet, china, friends, garter, shoes, dresses, church, license, cookbook, wedding plans, Mr. and Mrs., ring pillow, trousseau, announcements, justice of the peace, etc.

Be sure to put a "free" space in the middle. After you make out the cards, make yourself a master list of the words used. Cut them apart and put in a container you can shake. Then pick out one word at a time, calling them aloud just as in Bingo. Use poker chips, buttons, pieces of paper with wedding rings drawn on them, or make little loops of cord.

Play four corners, lines, fill the card or whatever type of game you like. The person that completes the specified game shouts "Bride".

— Entries too numerous to mention

Bingo Scoring Potpourri

By Carol Wolf, Union Grove, Wisconsin

AFTER you play bride (or baby) bingo, use this method to figure out the winning score. (Be sure to pass out paper and pencils for your guests to do the figuring.)

Write down the score of the person to your left (how many squares she has covered). Count how many squares on your own card are covered, and add to your score sheet.

Add the number of covered squares the bride has on her card. Count how many you have *uncovered* on your card, and subtract them from your score.

Anyone present whose wedding anniversary falls in the same month as the bride's future wedding day? If so, she should add 50 points to her score.

Subtract the score of the person on your right (number of squares covered). Add the bride's mother's score. Add the bridegroom's mother's score. Total. High score wins.

Matching Bingo

By Mrs. Glenn Tedrow, Fairfield, Iowa

HAVE BLANK bingo cards ready, with spaces marked off for your guests. Ask each guest to silently write in the names of kitchen utensils or gadgets on her card, filling each space.

Then go around the room and have each guest read off the items listed on her card. Everyone in the room should then place a button or other marker on their card where they have the same item listed. Play just as you would regular bingo, filling cards, lines, corners or whatever.

Wishing Well Game

By Mildred Grenier, St. Joseph, Missouri

GUESTS SIT in a circle. The first guest must say to the bride-to-be, "I wish for you_____" and name something starting with the letter "A". Allow about 10 seconds. The next guest must wish for the bride something starting with the letter "B", the next guest names something starting with the letter "C", and so on.

Name some comical things as well as serious things, such as "I wish for you ants in your pantry," or "I wish for you beauty when you get up in the morning," etc. If one cannot think of a thing to name in 10 seconds, she must drop out of the game. The one who remains in the game the longest wins.

Rings

By Mrs. Glenn Tedrow, Fairfield, Iowa

It started with a little ring.
  'Twas on the telephone.
But soon there was a diamond
  That was my very own.
Before so many months had passed
  We vowed that we'd be two,
And from that day a wedding ring
  Was on my finger too.
A year has flown and now we have
  The cutest wee-living thing—
Big eyes, some curls and dimples too,
  All caused by little rings.

Ah, Marriage!

Here's another fill-in-the-space game that's guaranteed to bring on laughter!

By Virginia Kaska, Atalissa, Iowa

GIVE EACH guest a sheet of paper, and have them write the bride's name down the left hand side as shown, and these headings across the top: Grocery Item, Furniture, Honeymoon Site, Household Chore and Wearing Apparel.

Allow five minutes for each guest to fill in the blanks, and then read them aloud.

	Grocery Item	Furniture	Honeymoon Site	Household Chore	Wearing Apparel
D	Donuts	Desk	Des Moines	Dusting	Driving Gloves
E	Eggs	End Table	England	Empty Trash	Earrings
B	Broccoli	Bed	Bermuda	Burn Leaves	Bra
R	Rice	Rocker	Rochester	Re-potting	Rings
A	Apples	Arm Chair	Alaska	Accounting	Ascot

Blank Fever

EACH GUEST may play alone, or work with someone as a team. Provide paper and pencils for your guests. (Prepare the sheets ahead of time, or let the guests make their own.) Turn the paper horizontally and write the word "corsage" (or something related to weddings) across the top, leaving a space between each letter.

In the margin on the left, write these categories: Honeymoon Spots (names of cities), Kitchen Utensils (or appliances), Soaps (or cleansers), Cooking Spices, and Bridegroom's Favorite Foods. Or, use your imagination and make other categories of your own.

Fill in the blank spaces with an appropriate answer for each category, using a word beginning with the letter at the top of the column.

Guests may either read their answers aloud, or the hostess may. Tell your guests not to use the same word twice—that takes even more thinking!!

Here's a sample sheet:

—Entries too numerous to mention

	C	**O**	**R**	**S**	**A**	**G**	**E**
Honeymoon Spots:	Chicago	Ozarks	Rio	San Francisco	Alps	Germany	Europe
Kitchen Utensils (or appliances):	colander	oven	refrigerator	spoon	apple corer	grinder	egg beater
Bridegroom's Favorite Foods:	chili	omelets	rice	spaghetti	apple pie	gravy	escargo
Soaps:	Cheer	Oxydol	Rinso Blue	Salvo	Ajax	Gain	Era
Cooking Spices:	chives	oregano	rosemary	sage	anise	ginger	elecampane aniseed

Bridal Bowling

By Ann Brower, Keota, Iowa

DIVIDE THE shower guests into two equal groups and have them stand in rows facing each other.

Give the person at the head of each line a bowl containing a number of items. Be sure to have identical items in each bowl. Give the person at the opposite end of each line a large paper sack. At the word "GO", the leaders should each take one item at a time from the bowl and pass it to the next in line.

When the person at the foot of the line gets the items, she should place them in the paper sack. When all items have been passed and placed in the sack, the sack is *passed* back up the line to the lead person.

Now, the guests will likely think this ends the game, with the first line finished as the winner. Not so! Now give each guest paper and pencil, and instruct them to each write down what items were passed! The one with the most correct items is the winner.

Score by giving one point for each correct item or, if you want to penalize players for just guessing, give one point for each correct answer, and deduct two points for each "guess".

Door Prize Warm Ups

By Mrs. Eugene Placek, Western, Nebraska

ONE GOOD way to distribute door prizes is to tape a card or two under several chairs in the room. At some point in the shower, have the guests check their chairs, and the people with a card get a prize.

Let's Get Acquainted!

This is an especially good game to get to know the bride-to-be and also the guests.

By Laurie Norris, Hesperia, Michigan

HAVE EACH person number her paper from 1-12. Then as you ask your guests what their "favorite" is, have them write their personal answers.

When all 12 favorites have been asked, have the bride-to-be tell what her 12 favorites are. The person with the most answers matching the bride's, receives the prize.

What is Your Favorite:

1. color
2. pie
3. season
4. flower
5. number
6. song
7. beverage
8. holiday
9. singer
10. car
11. television program
12. ice cream

Guess the Guests

By Mrs. Eugene Placek, Western, Nebraska

WHEN YOU'VE invited your guests, start making up questions about them so that sometime during the shower, you can ask the ladies present each of the questions. Let them match each question with the correct person.

Example: Which woman here shares her name with a flower? (Rose)

Which lady's name do you use before meals? (Grace)

Which lady will sigh deeply the day after the (or give specific date) wedding? (The name of the bride's mother).

Eavesdropping on the Bride

By Janet Toews, Penalosa, Kansas

WHILE THE bride-to-be is opening her gifts, have someone sit nearby and inconspicuously take down snatches of her comments while she's unwrapping. Example: ("Oh, wow," "How neat," "Oh, I've always wanted one of these," etc.) After the gifts are open, read her remarks to the guests.

Poet in the House?

By Joy Ann Hayman, Veedersburg, Indiana

IF POSSIBLE, have a friend or relative of the bride write a comical, original poem depicting the events in the bride's life and the romance that led to her engagement. Read the poem aloud.

Bottled Advice

By Mrs. Glenn Tedrow, Fairfield, Iowa

HAVE YOUR SHOWER guests write some advice on little bits of paper, and place them in a large pill bottle. The bride-to-be will have plenty of picker-uppers for a little one-a-day reading.

Pack Her Suitcase!

By Mrs. Clifford Johnson, Owatonna, Minnesota

BEFORE THE shower, pack a small suitcase with things a bride (or mother-to-be) would need on her honeymoon (or at the hospital). Before showing the guests the contents, allow five minutes for each to write down what she *thinks* might be inside.

Have the guest of honor open the bag and, one at a time, take the items out. The person with the most correct, wins. (Some suggestions: Panty hose, toothbrush, bra, toothpaste, nightie, makeup, safety pins, nail polish, hair spray, etc. Be sure to pack something silly—like a teddy bear.)

Workbasket Game

By Mrs. Clifford Johnson, Owatonna, Minnesota

PLACE objects commonly found in a workbasket into a bag or workbasket (about 20-25 items). Pass around the room, hide it from view, and have the guests list as many as they can remember. Here are a few suggestions: Thread, tape, yarn, bobbin, pin, needles, elastic, bias tape, pincushion, scissors, emery board, embroidery thread, cord, ruler, thimble, patterns, buttons, ribbon, safety pin, etc.

Match the Proverbs

Make sure there's room for active trading with this fun game!

By Mildred Grenier, St. Joseph, Missouri

TYPE THESE proverbs about love and marriage on strips of paper, then cut each strip in half and mix. Give each guest a strip and instruct them to trade with the other guests, until their proverb is correctly completed. The one who first completes her proverb is the winner.

1. Absence makes/the heart grow fonder.
2. Love/casts out fear.
3. It is better/to have loved and lost, than not to have loved at all.
4. All the world/loves a lover.
5. All's fair/in love and war.
6. Faint heart/never won fair lady.
7. True love never/runs smooth.
8. Two can live/as cheaply as one.
9. Love/is blind.
10. Love gives itself—it is not bought.
11. If there is anything better than to be loved,/it is loving.
12. He who falls in love with himself/will have no rivals.

Questions and Answers?

By Mrs. Elroy Jensen, Canby, Minnesota

GIVE EACH guest a pencil and two slips of paper. On one, the guests should write a question a bride might ask, and on the other, the answer to that question. Then collect all the questions and place in one bag, and all the answers, placing them in another bag. Give both bags a good shake.

Pass both bags around, and have each guest select one question and one answer, reading them aloud to everyone. Needless to say, the results are hilarious.

Bride's Art Class

By Mrs. Rodney Voelker, Brownsdale, Minnesota

GIVE EACH guest a piece of paper and pencil. Each must place the paper on top of her head and try to draw a picture of a bride. The honored guest picks out the best one and the person who drew it wins a prize.

Cotton Scoop-Up

By Mrs. Rodney Voelker, Brownsdale, Minnesota

PUT SOME cotton balls on a card table. Place an empty bowl in front of a person who is sitting at the table blindfolded. Give her a spoon and have her try to scoop up cotton balls with the spoon and put them in the bowl. Allow about a minute for each guest and the one who scoops the most cotton balls into the bowl wins a prize.

Wedding Day Advice

By Mary Dallmann, North Lake, Wisconsin

PASS OUT sheets of paper to your guests, and ask them to write "A bridegroom should always..." across the top. On the left margin, ask them to write the letters "groom" from top to bottom.

Then ask them to write words of advice (funny or serious) in the spaces, using phrases that use words starting with "g", "r", etc. Have your guests read them aloud to each other when finished.

Advice for the Bride

By Anna Mary Yoder, Middlebury, Indiana

HAVE EACH guest write down a suggestion for the bride, such as "Never go to bed angry at each other" or "Keep interests of your own as well as those your husband is interested in."

Have each guest read hers aloud—some may be humorous too! Then give them to the bride-to-be as a momento.

More Advice

By Roylinda Rumbaugh, Mattawan, Michigan

ANOTHER variation of the advice game is to give each guest about 10 minutes to write a short letter of advice to the bride. Seal them in an envelope and tell her to read them after her honeymoon.

Recipe Interpretation

A game for gourmet cooks!

By Erma Reynolds, Longmeadow, Massachusetts

BEFORE THE shower, check a cookbook and select unusual recipes, making certain the directions do not mention the recipe's title.

Number each recipe, and put slips of paper in the cookbook, noting the location of each.

At game time, pass out pencil and paper. Each guest in turn opens to a marked section in the cookbook, and announces the recipe's number, but not its title. Then she reads the recipe, while the other players try to name the recipe, noting its name by the corresponding number on their paper. Remove slip when reading is finished.

When everyone has had a turn, the player with the longest, most correct list wins. (Examples: guacamole, schweizerschnitzel, spoon bread, lord baltimore cake, divinity fudge, blancmange, fruit cobbler, sauerbraten, philadelphia scrapple, lasagne, chef's salad, borsch.)

ABC's of Cooking

By Charlotte Roach, Faucett, Missouri

THIS GAME can be played two ways—either as a pencil and paper game, with players working individually, or have your guests sit in a circle and answer the questions in turn. If you use paper and pencil, the person who gets the most correct answers, wins. If you use the "circle" method, when a person can't answer the question, she is out.

Have your guests name something found in the kitchen, beginning with each letter of the alphabet: A-Apron, B-Broom, C-Can Opener, etc. If necessary repeat the alphabet until only one person is left (in the case of the circle method).

Name the Love Song

By Mrs. Rodney Voelker, Brownsdale, Minnesota

IF YOU have a piano and a collection of romantic or wedding-related songs, play a few bars of each and have your guests try to identify them by writing their guesses on paper. The one with the most correct wins.

How Did You Meet?

By Mrs. Randa Nill, Kulm, North Dakota

A FUN little mixer is to have each guest share briefly the story of how she and her husband first met. There are some really funny tales.

What Am I?

By Mrs. Rodney Voelker, Brownsdale, Minnesota

FOR A kitchen shower, make a card for each guest bearing the names of common kitchen utensils, such as frying pan, tea kettle, spatula, beater, etc. When it's time for the game, pin a card on the back of each guest. Each person must ask questions of the others until she learns what is printed on the tag on her back. Such questions asked could be "What am I made of?" or "Am I used for cooking?" etc.

Cooking Term Quiz

By Erma Reynolds, Longmeadow, Massachusetts

WHEN ALL the guests have arrived, pin a slip of paper on the back of each person with a cooking term—with the vowels missing in the spelling of each word. Pass out paper and pencils.

At your signal the players begin to read each other's slips, trying to decipher each one. At the end of seven minutes, player with longest, most correct list, wins a prize. Examples: k n d (knead), f r s t (frost), g r n s h (garnish), j l n n (julienne), f l l t (fillet), f l k (flake), f r c s s (fricassee), s c l d (scald), s l v r (sliver), r s t (roast), p r b l (parboil), m r n d (marinade), etc.

Greatest Cooking Failures

By Mrs. Eugene Placek, Western, Nebraska

TAKE A couple of minutes to have your guests describe the greatest cooking disasters during their marriages. It could be hilarious!

Tissue Tattletales

Here's a great game to make the bride feel at ease.

By Ann Brower, Keota, Iowa

THIS IS a game where everyone participates and the challenge is lots of fun. But don't give your "secret" away until the tissue is passed out.

Pass around a roll of pink toilet tissue (or some other appropriate color), instructing each guest to tear off "the usual amount".

After all guests have their tissue, advise them that they are each to create a bridal corsage, using the exact amount of tissue they have taken. Some will have a reasonable amount, others will have only one small square, and others an enormous over-ample amount. They may tear, fold, twist, tie or anything else to form a corsage, but each must limit it to the amount of tissue they have.

Judge the corsages, award prizes to the winners. You might want to pick several winners, if the crowd is large. Have different categories, such as most beautiful, most realistic, most ridiculous, etc.

Another Toilet Paper Game

By Anita Sue Yoder, Middlebury, Indiana

PASS A roll of toilet paper and ask your guests to tear off what they'll need. Don't let them know what they'll need it for.

Now tell the guests they must design a wedding dress for the bride with their toilet paper. Provide straight pins, bobby pins and scotch tape so they can attach the paper to the bride-to-be's clothing and hair.

Bridal Garters

By Carol Wolf, Union Grove, Wisconsin

MAKE EACH of your guests a tiny garter, using narrow elastic and light blue crepe paper. Give one to each as they come in and tell them they must wear it. (Some are embarrassed and want to go into another room to put it on. Others wear the garters on their ankles!)

Make even tinier garters for napkin holders, using the narrowest elastic you can find, and narrow satin ribbon. Make one of them pink...that person gets the door prize!

Balloon Break

By Mrs. Frank Dehaas, Greencreek, Idaho

THIS IS a good ice-breaker. Give each guest a blown up balloon. Inside one, place a slip of paper. The person who finds the slip of paper, wins a door prize. To break the balloons, guests must sit on them.

Dress the Bride

DIVIDE YOUR shower guests into groups of five or six. If possible, send them into separate rooms with equal amounts of toilet tissue (or tissue paper), straight pins, bobby pins, and tape.

Have each group select one person to be the "bride". Allow them 5-10 minutes to design and make a gown for their bride—making dress, veil, train, bouquets, etc. The group with the most original and "beautiful" bride's gown wins.

—Entries too numerous to mention

Modeling Job

By Laurie Norris, Hesperia, Michigan

PURCHASE or make two corsages. Place both in a box and wrap with appropriate wrapping paper.

To introduce the game to your guests, you might say: "Since we are fairly well acquainted and there are no men present, we thought that perhaps two of you ladies would like to model a little something for the rest of us."

Try to create a little suspense and fear in the minds of the other guests. Explain that one of the models will be the bride-to-be herself. Start a timer and have the guests pass the box around the circle from lady to lady. When the timer rings, whoever is holding the box must model its contents.

This is a fun game because the ladies are so sure the box contains some personal attire they are eager to pass the box to the next lady.

Also, the corsage is a nice way of recognizing your guest of honor.

Instead of two corsages, you could purchase a necklace or scarf for the guest who models. Or, you may arrange it so that the timer rings when the groom's mother has the box, as special recognition for her.

What Was That?

Here's a fun memory game.

By Mrs. Martin Covert, Sandwich, Illinois

PLACE AS many items on a tray as you have guests at your shower. Suggestions are: baby powder, lotion, a small hand towel, a hot mitt, tiny bottle of cologne, stationery, etc.

Put each of the guests' names into a fishbowl six times. Number the guests off and make sure everyone knows everyone else's first name.

As each name is drawn from the fishbowl, have that person take an item from the tray, continuing until all are taken. Each person should hide the article behind herself.

Then as names are drawn again, the person called must give the name and number *and* remember the article of a person who has an article she'd like. If she's right, she receives the other person's item, and if not, nothing changes. When all the names have been called around, the people holding the articles may keep them—or give them to the bride. This game is a good mixer. Play several rounds.

Find the Clue Gift Game

By Janet Toews, Penalosa, Kansas

BEFORE THE shower, glue a tiny piece of paper with a number on it to a cotton ball, making one for each guest you expect to attend. As the guests arrive, give a cotton ball to each of them. Place corresponding numbers on each gift, using little cards.

When it is time to open presents, send the bride out of the room and ask each guest to hide her cotton ball.

Have the bride find a cotton ball, and then open the matching numbered gift.

Tricky Clothespins

By Mrs. Mark Nill, Kulm, North Dakota

AT THE beginning of the shower, give each guest a clothespin. Tell all to attach theirs to the hem of either their slacks or skirt. Then tell all of them *not* to cross their legs.

Anyone who crosses her legs loses her clothespin to the first person who sees it. The person with the most clothespins at the end of the shower gets a prize (how about a clothespin bag?), which she gives to the bride, along with all the clothespins.

A Note to the Hostess

By Bonnie Gazdag, Kalamazoo, Michigan

IF A SHOWER is being given in your honor (and it's not a surprise), take the hostess a little something to say "thank you". Or send it later. She and her helpers have done a lot to give you a special day.

Gift Scavenger Hunt

By Estelle Salata, Hamilton, Ontario

BEFORE THE bride opens her gifts, give her a gaily decorated box, or a shiny copper kettle, filled with slips of paper. On each slip of paper write the location, in riddle form, of one of her presents.

Here's an example: (Tuck the gift in a cedar chest.)
"From the forests of Lebanon comes my wood,
Just open the lid and peek under the hood."
Here is a clue for a gift hidden in the refrigerator:
"I'm locked in the cooler,
It's thirty degrees,
Please rescue me quickly
Before I freeze."

Bridal Fortune-telling

By Esther Fahning, Wells, Minnesota

WRAP VARIOUS articles and place them in a shopping bag. Have each guest select one, and taking turns, unwrap them. As they unwrap the item, read their "fortune". Here are some suggestions:
Glove: She'll decline a proposal.
Rice: She'll be married next.
Ruler: She'll marry a teacher.
Coin: She'll come into money.
Envelope: Good news soon.
Stamp: His family will approve.
Clock: She'll have to be more prompt.
Bobby Pin: His name will be Bob.
Pencil: She'll become an author, etc.

Matrimony Mix-ups

Exercise your word power with this fun little mix-up!

By Laurie Norris, Hesperia, Michigan

UNSCRAMBLE THESE words:

Courtship:

midnoda (diamond)
fecwru (curfew)
enyrodbif (boyfriend)
teasd (dates)
ogngi detays (going steady)
apler (pearl)
sacls nirg (class ring)
sksi (kiss)
dohl nadsh (hold hands)
becamer (embrace)

Wedding:

cumis (music)
gnir reabre (ring bearer)
daeclsn (candles)
natandestt (attendants)
rimenist (minister)
losstio (soloist)
urnren (runner)

elfrows (flowers)
dextou (tuxedo)
wogn (gown)

Trousseau:

naypt oshe (panty hose)
legineeg (negligee)
danricag (cardigan)
tipsanut (pantsuit)
facrs (scarf)
regileni (lingerie)
esulob (blouse)
vosleg (gloves)
tobos (boots)
eajctk (jacket)

Reception:

sugets (guests)
gropehartpoh (photographer)
hucpn (punch)
esnpters (presents)
eci mecar (ice cream)
wohtr retrga (throw garter)
cetidranoso (decorations)
cire (rice)
acek (cake)
pinsank (napkins)

Marriage Unscramble

By Mrs. Marcel Nechanicky, Buckingham, Iowa

1. a fost reswan (a soft answer)
2. evas a nepny (save a penny)
3. epek glinims (keep smiling)
4. veah centipae (have patience)
5. vase nad vahe (save and have)
6. gluah a tlo (laugh a lot)
7. kinth phypa shoutthg (think happy thoughts)
8. evol dan be devol (love and be loved)
9. ctarpice densinks (practice kindness)
10. sendskin spay (kindness pays)
11. eb no mite (be on time)
12. aveh rougeca (have courage)
13. a miles shelp (a smile helps)
14. leary ot deb (early to bed)
15. yeral ot sire (early to rise)
16. od ton worth toness (do not throw stones)
17. pleedvo sepio (develop poise)
18. kame theas owlyls (make haste slowly)
19. gins a gons (sing a song)

Kitchen Scramble

By Mrs. Rodney Voelker, Brownsdale, Minnesota

1. atsualp (spatula)
2. enlerbd (blender)
3. hsdewhiasr (dishwasher)
4. rrgtoarfriee (refrigerator)
5. asrtote (toaster)
6. fnike (knife)
7. acn eprneo (can opener)
8. rasotre (roaster)
9. isosrirete (rotisserie)
10. osnop (spoon)
11. ikoceo ajr (cookie jar)
12. ehortmrteem (thermometer)
13. otvse (stove)
14. rfko (fork)
15. remix (mixer)
16. akce nap (cake pan)
17. umignesra opons (measuring spoon)
18. tegarr (grater)

Wedding Preparations

Here's what the bride and groom should have ready for the big day!

By Mildred Grenier, St. Joseph, Missouri

UNSCRAMBLE THESE words to find out what (bride's name) and (bridegroom's name) need for the wedding.

1. sitinonavit — (invitations)
2. sinkpan — (napkins)
3. chunp — (punch)
4. kace — (cake)
5. tobequu — (bouquet)
6. wong — (gown)
7. deardimbiss — (bridesmaids)
8. figst — (gifts)
9. cire — (rice)
10. eachrerp — (preacher)
11. toilsos — (soloist)
12. hurchc — (church)
13. ginddew singr — (wedding rings)
14. tebs nam — (best man)
15. heynoonmo — (honeymoon)
16. sinceel — (license)
17. xepenses — (expenses)
18. indwged hamrc — (wedding march)
19. tengmangee nigr — (engagement ring)
20. solaprop — (proposal)

Hearts

By Mildred Grenier, St. Joseph, Missouri

COMPLETE EACH description with a word that starts with "heart".

1. Sorrow, grief (heartache)
2. Acidity of the stomach (heartburn)
3. To give courage to (hearten)
4. Sincere, earnest (heartfelt)
5. That part of the room where fire is made (hearth)
6. Cordially (heartily)
7. Without feeling (heartless)
8. Causing grief (heartrending)
9. The pansy (heartsease)
10. Cordial (hearty)

What Age?

By Mrs. Frank Dehaas, Greencreek, Idaho

FILL IN the blanks with words that end with the suffix "age".

John fell in love with Sue and decided to ask her hand in (marri)age. But lacking (cour)age, he was forced to write to her. His only (post)age stamp would not stick, so he borrowed some (mucil)age and said, "I must (man)age and not (dam)age my clothes with it."

Sue's answer to his letter was "My hero, all (hom)age to you." Send your (carri)age for my (lugg)age and meet me at the (parson)age with plenty of (coin)age. For their wedding breakfast, the had (saus)age and (cabb)age. They lived in a (cott)age until their (old) age.

Wedding Flowers

By Mrs. Rodney Voelker, Brownsdale, Minnesota

COMPLETE each description with the name of a flower.

1. The bride's name, with color of her hair (Marigold).
2. The color of her eyes (Violet).
3. Her bridegroom's name and what she called him (Sweet William).
4. The candy he took his bride (Candytuft).
5. The time he serenaded her (Four-O'-Clocks).
6. The instrument he used (Trumpet).
7. What the bride's father punished the bridegroom with (Golden Rod).
8. What the bridegroom did (Balsam).
9. What the bridegroom did when he proposed (Aster).
10. To whom did she refer him for an answer? (Poppy).
11. What flower did he first press? (Tulips).
12. The minister who married them (Jack-in-the-Pulpit).
13. What he hoped for their happiness (Everlasting Straw Flowers).
14. What the bridegroom said when he went away from his bride (Forget-me-not).
15. The name of the first baby (Baby's Breath).
16. What hallowed their declining years (Sweet Pea).
17. What she shopped at the market for (Butter-and-Eggs).
18. What the weather was like on the couple's wedding day (Morning Glory, Sunflower).
19. Name of the little ring bearer (Johnny Jump Up).

The Bride Takes the Cake

Something deliciously different!

By Mrs. Martin Covert, Sandwich, Illinois

WHEN THE BRIDE gets married, she'll be baking lots of cakes. See how many kinds you can list, using the following descriptions:

1. The cake like the precious metal (gold).
2. Something to tie in your hair (ribbon).
3. Found on the ocean floor (sponge).
4. It's a small kid's game (marble).
5. We get this from a tall tree (coconut).
6. A typical American breakfast (coffee).
7. A heavenly body (angel food).
8. As lovely as this transparent fabric (chiffon).
9. Dishes (cupcakes).
10. There is a pot of gold at the end of the (rainbow).
11. An un-heavenly body (devil's food).
12. Make the bottom the top (upside down).
13. Always on the calendar (date).
14. Baseball players do this (bundt).
15. To go crazy (banana).
16. A common color at Halloween (orange).
17. A "bad" bargain (lemon).
18. Used in a certain game (checkerboard).
19. We put this on a bed (sheet).
20. To be sad, and, associated with Adam and Eve (pineapple).

Know the Bride

PASS OUT paper and pencils to your guests, and ask the bride to leave the room. The one with the most correct answers to the following questions, wins. Allow 5-10 minutes. Use all or part of the list.

1. What color shoes does she have on?
2. Is her diamond set in white or yellow gold?
3. When is her wedding date?
4. What is the name of her fiance?
5. What are the bride's colors for her wedding?
6. What color dress is she wearing today?
7. How tall is the bride?
8. What color is her hair?
9. What is her fiance's occupation?
10. Does the bride-to-be have a watch on?
11. What color is her slip?
12. What is her approximate weight?
13. How did the couple meet?
14. Where will they live?
15. What kind of car do they have?
16. What is the bride's favorite color?
17. What is her favorite meat?
18. What is her favorite flower?
19. What is her favorite sport?
20. What is her favorite place to visit?
21. What kind of music does she like best?
22. What was her favorite subject in school?
23. What is her favorite month of the year?
24. What nationality of food is her favorite?
25. What is her favorite leisure time activity?
26. What is her favorite perfume?
27. What is her favorite new song?
28. What would be her choice of a pet?
29. What is her favorite flavor of ice cream?

— *Entries too numerous to mention.*

Famous Lovers Game

By Mildred Grenier, St. Joseph, Missouri

TYPE THE names of these famous lovers on a piece of paper for each guest. Have your guests match the names in the first column with the names in the second column. The one who correctly matches the most names gets the prize.

1. Juliet (j)	a. Gabriel
2. Bess (i)	b. Reuben
3. Cleopatra (d)	c. George
4. Mamie (e)	d. Anthony
5. Rachel (b)	e. Ike
6. Rebekah (g)	f. Boaz
7. Scarlett (h)	g. Isaac
8. Evangeline (a)	h. Rhett
9. Martha (c)	i. Porgy
10. Ruth (f)	j. Romeo

Brand Name Game

By Mrs. David Brause, Bucyrus, Ohio

SPEND SOME time before the shower cutting out magazine advertisements for soaps, mattresses, and other products. Cover the words that spell out the brand name. Place a number on each page.

At the shower, ask your guests to number their papers, and start passing around the pictures. Guests should write down what they think the brand name is—Duncan Hines, Betty Crocker, etc. The person with the most correct names, wins.

First Name Game

Men's and women's first names are the answers in this pencil and paper game.

By Mrs. William J. Schmidt, Randolph, Wisconsin

WRITE IN THE first name best describing the following:

1. To wed (Mary)
2. Article used before words beginning with a vowel (Ann)
3. A sound amplifier (Mike)
4. What hippies are (Harry)
5. A detective (Dick)
6. A month of the year (April, May, June, or August)
7. A Christmas song (Carol)
8. A type of hay (Timothy)
9. A room for athletic events (Jim)
10. A letter of the alphabet (Bea, Dee, Jay or Kay)
11. The winner (Victor)
12. A holiday drink (Tom & Jerry)
13. A college official (Dean)
14. A type of alcohol (Ethel)
15. Bring civil action against (Sue)
16. Sincere (Ernest)
17. A flowering shrub (Rose)
18. A messenger or forerunner (Harold)
19. A German coin (Mark)
20. A valley (Dale)
21. Device for raising a car (Jack)
22. The beginning of morning (Dawn)
23. To bend the joint between the leg and thigh (Neil)

Initials Game

By Mrs. Martin Covert, Sandwich, Illinois

TELL EACH GUEST to answer the questions you read, using their first and last name initials as the beginning of the words. Ask them to write their answers down, and then read them aloud later.

Example: If Jane Curtis was a shower guest, all her answers would have to be two words starting with J. and C.

1. What is your favorite food?
2. When are you the most romantic?
3. What kind of man attracts you?
4. What are your favorite pastimes?
5. What do you expect in a husband?
6. What are you afraid of?
7. How do you feel about kissing on the first date?
8. If you could be anyone in the world, besides yourself, who would that person be?
9. What is your greatest hope?
10. What makes you lose your temper?
11. Why should a husband fix his own breakfast?
12. Where would you like to spend your honeymoon?
13. Why should a husband help around the house?
14. What is your pet peeve?
15. What is your greatest personal quality?

Sweet Nothings

By Heather Lambrecht, Maple Valley, Washington

ASK YOUR GUESTS to number their papers 1-20 and one by one, read the following descriptions. The answer in each case is the name of a candy bar.

1. A trio of old (Three Musketeers)
2. Sneering giggles (Snickers)
3. Charlie Brown's tomboy friend (Peppermint Patty)
4. A very large amount of money ($100,000 Bar)
5. One of the galaxies (Milky Way)
6. A snapping noise (Krackle)
7. A famous baseball player's name (Baby Ruth)
8. A clumsy person is sometimes called this (Butterfinger)
9. A famous American author (Oh Henry)
10. The red planet (Mars)
11. A kind of soft drink (7-Up)
12. A stoney street (Rocky Road)
13. A famous potato (Idaho Spud)
14. A romantic closing to a love letter (Forever Yours)
15. A famous street in New York (5th Avenue)
16. Twin letters (M&M's)

Spring Ride

Here's a game sure to create a house full of laughter.

By Mrs. Clifford Johnson, Owatonna, Minnesota

DUPLICATE THE following poem, leaving blanks where the answers are now shown. Give your shower guests 5-10 minutes to fill in the words related to automobiles and the bride's ride with a former beau one fine spring day. Use the bride's name in the verse where needed.

"(Bride's name) and her beau one day, went riding in his Chevrolet. Her beau was fat, his name was Frank, and he was somewhat of a (crank). It was too bad he wasn't smarter, but he couldn't work the (starter). She showed him how, the little dear, and also how to shift the (gear). Away they went, but something broke, 'Twas just a measly little (spoke). He fixed it with a piece of wire, then something popped—it was a (tire).

" 'Twas mended soon, but next ker-plop, they struck a branch and smashed the (top). 'Dear me', said (bride's name), 'That's too much!' Then something happened to the (clutch). And next, poor Frank, unlucky dud, just grazed a rock and smashed a (hub). They crossed a brook but missed the ford, and sank down to the (running board). 'Oh Frank', cried (bride), with a squeal, 'I think we're going to lose a (wheel). They climbed a hill, and then 'twas seen, the tank contained no (gasoline). They coasted downward toward the lake, but Frankie couldn't work the (brake). They struck a post a moment later, that almost wrecked the (radiator). So both climbed out, and poor old Frank, bought gasoline and filled the (tank). And gathered up from road and field, the remnants of the broken (shield). They fixed the engine tight and snug, and, had to use a new (spark plug). Just then he slapped a mosquito, and dropped a wrench on the (magneto). 'Twas useless then to sweat and toil, nothing would run except the (oil). They journeyed home with Frankie pushin', while (bride) sobbed upon a (cushion). So poor Frankie's hopes were doomed to (blight), (or word to rhyme with bridegroom's name) and (bride's name) married (bridegroom).''

Meet the Happy Couple

By Mrs. Jack McCullough, Sharon, Wisconsin

HERE'S A GOOD game to help your guests learn a little more about the new couple—so often people know either the bride or groom but not both. When the game is finished, everyone will feel like they know both of them much better.

Pass out paper and pencils. Read the following questions, using the correct names and allowing time for your guests to answer.

1. How did _____ and _____ meet?
      (bride's name)   (bridegroom's name)

2. What is the date of their wedding?
3. When is the bride's birthday?
4. What time will the wedding begin?
5. Where will they live?
6. When is the bridegroom's birthday?
7. Where does the bride work?
8. Who are the bridesmaids?
9. Where did the bride and bridegroom meet?
10. Where does the bridegroom work?
11. What school did the bride graduate from?
12. Who are the ushers?
13. The wedding colors will be_____?
14. What high school did the bridegroom graduate from?
15. The bride's new in-laws are_____and _____.
16. The bridegroom's new in-laws are _____and_____.
17. Where will the wedding take place?
18. Where will the reception take place?
19. Where will the bride and bridegroom be going for their honeymoon?

The bride can respond to any "unanswered" questions—but don't expect her to tell you about Number 19!

Utensil Mysteries

By Mildred Grenier, St. Joseph, Missouri

HAVE SMALL kitchen gadgets, such as a cheese slicer, egg poacher, wire whisk, bottle opener, bottle capper, potato slicer, etc., tied in cloth or paper bags. Number the bags and keep a list for yourself. Pass them around, letting each guest feel each bag and guess what is inside. The one who guesses the largest number wins. Answers should be written.

The Busy Homemaker

Tell your guests to fill in the blanks with words common around the house or the kitchen.

By Marge Wenzel, Kent, Illinois

1. The bride made (tea towels) for her hope chest.
2. Her bouquet consisted of (sweet peas) and (corn flowers).
3. They went to (china) on their honeymoon.
4. One day the groom came home and found his bride in the kitchen. She told him she was (bacon) a cake.
5. In a few minutes it burned and she shed (salty) tears.
6. Then he used (peppery) words in giving his opinion of anyone doing such a thing.
7. She threatened to leave him and called him an (egg) head.
8. But then he said, "I (steak) my life on you."
9. And she felt much (butter).
10. He said, "Let us (hop) for I must (prune) the trees."
11. She looked at him and said, "We are a happy (pear) again, aren't we, dear?"
12. And he said, "We are the best (match) in town."

Kitchen Riddles

By Mrs. Frank Dehaas, Greencreek, Idaho

AFTER PLAYING, give the named kitchen items to the bride-to-be.
1. What a husband should not do to his wife (beater)
2. What is used in the harvest field? (fork)
3. What you receive when you fall (a jar)
4. What lovers do in the moonlight (spoon)
5. An important man in baseball games (pitcher)
6. How do you look after a fall? (pail)
7. A conceited ladies' man (spud masher)
8. Belonging to a fish (scales)
9. Mrs. Jiggs's best friend (rolling pin)
10. Flowers grow in (pots)

Another Kitchen Scramble

By Beth Tobler, Appleton, Wisconsin

UNSCRAMBLE THESE kitchen words. The person with the most correct after 10 minutes, wins.

1. dtcuh eovn	(dutch oven)
2. xmire	(mixer)
3. opoatt elpere	(potato peeler)
4. rbelnde	(blender)
5. lirolgn npi	(rolling pin)
6. sparty ubsrh	(pastry brush)
7. oaedclrn	(colander)
8. oeattsr	(toaster)
9. lirbroe	(broiler)
10. sehrma	(masher)
11. aictrnse	(canister)

Gourmet Unscramble

By Mrs. Francis Show, Mill Run, Pennsylvania

HERE are a few suggested words to unscramble:

nprliabo	(panbroil)
esesfrica	(fricassee)
chbnla	(blanch)
asebir	(braise)
zlceraaiem	(caramelize)
mcera	(cream)
vledssoi	(dissolve)
lzgae	(glaze)
terag	(grate)
denka	(knead)
aatemnir	(marinate)
hpaoc	(poach)
sutea	(saute)
pwhi	(whip)
rmsmei	(simmer)
hrdse	(shred)
cmnei	(mince)
kproeoc	(precook)
rbeda	(bread)
hlcli	(chill)

Supermarket Slogans

Michell Talbert, Vandalia, Missouri

ANOTHER WAY to play the brand names game is to read aloud slogans (all or in part) and have your guests write down the product name.

Example: "So squeezably soft, it's irresistible" (Charmin bathroom tissue).

Honeymoon Hash

Silly advice—this will make everybody laugh!

By Judy Gerth, Princeton, Minnesota

FILL IN the spaces below with fruits and vegetables selected from this master list—there are more than you'll need.

Apple	Grapes	Peppers
Avocado	Grapefruit	Plums
Bean	Mushroom	Pear
Beet	Limes	Peach
Banana	Lettuce	Pineapple
Broccoli	Olive	Raspberry
Cauliflower	Melon	Radish
Cabbage	Onion	Raisin
Carrot	Orange	Strawberry
Celery	Lemons	Spinach
Cucumber	Peas	Sauerkraut
Corn	Parsley	Tomato
Cantaloupe	Parsnip	Turnip
Dates	Prunes	

Dear (name) & (name):

Everyone gives advice to newlyweds, so why should we be an exception? First of all, as you know, you (cantaloupe) because everyone wants to see the wedding, and if you (carrot) all you'll (turnip) at the church.

You may get the (raspberry) at first, but then you're not such sour (grapes) that you can't take it.

To you (bridegroom's name), please take this advice: Never (beet) your wife. Remain as cool as a (cucumber). Remember she's a human (bean) and a darn cute (tomato). (Bride's name) may not be a (strawberry) blonde but she does have a (radish) tint to her hair, and you'll both make a (peach) of a (pear).

To you (bride's name), a good wife always has a good disposition. Never be (melon) choly. We are glad to see that (bridegroom's name) has a good job and hope he will soon get a big (raisin) (celery). In closing kids, (lettuce) say this may be a lot of (corn) and we're (plum) crazy or even full of (prunes) but we sincerely hope this (peach) of a (pear) will be blessed with five little (peppers). May you two spend all your (dates) together and be in love (olive) your life.

Signed,
I.M. Dumm, President
U.R. Too, Secretary

P.S. Kindly remember to do all your necking in the (mushroom).

Feeding Unexpected Guests

By Mrs. Glenn Tedrow, Fairfield, Iowa

FILL IN the blanks with a meal idea (bride's name) could use if (bridegroom's name) brought folks home unexpectedly one night. The phrase listed should give you a clue.

1. A taxicab driver (cabbage)
2. A jeweler (carrots)
3. A justice of the peace or marrying preacher (pears)
4. A real estate man (cottage cheese)
5. A traffic officer (jam)
6. A teacher (alphabet noodles)
7. An actor (ham)
8. Some newlyweds (lettuce alone)
9. Plumber (leeks)
10. An electrician (currants)
11. A shoemaker (sole)
12. A gambler (steaks)

"Something White" Game

By Jo Wenzel, Kent, Illinois

COLLECT AS MANY "white" things as you can in your kitchen and bath (detergent, lotion, flour, sugar, milk, etc.). Put samples in small paper cups or dishes. Number and mark each in some manner. About 20-25 items would be best.

Have your guests identify each, writing down the names on paper. Caution them that some may not taste very good and should be sniffed. The person with the most correct, wins. Be sure the prize is white, of course!

What's Inside?

By Carol Wolf, Union Grove, Wisconsin

BEFORE the shower, carefully pry a walnut apart. Inside, place rubber bands, or clips, pins, tacks, stamps, etc. and glue closed. Ask your guests to guess what is inside.

Guess the Food

Scout out the trickiest items you can find!

By Carla Read, Henry, Illinois

WRAP 7-10 food items and put a number on each package to identify it. Pass the items to your shower guests, and let them shake and feel the packages to guess what's inside. The person with the most correct answers wins a small prize—how about some special occasion paper napkins? The bride-to-be receives the food items.

Here are some suggestions: A box of pudding, can of soup, box of macaroni and cheese, a single envelope of whipped topping, box of jello, small box of raisins, tea bag, package of Kool Aid, cake mix, a spice, or a box of salt.

Cook's Choice

By Anne Olson, Muscatine, Iowa

MAKE 15 little cloth sacks, each with a finished measurement of about 1½- x 2½-inches. Mark each with numbers 1-15, using a permanent marking pen.

Fill each sack with a kitchen ingredient, and sew up the end so it won't leak. Make yourself a master list of which ingredient is in which bag.

(Use items like salt, pepper, sugar, flour, tapioca, cornstarch, baking soda, cocoa, baking soda, oatmeal, rice, etc.)

Have each guest number her paper 1-15. Pass the sacks, and let them feel and smell them to try to guess the contents. The person with the most correct answers, wins.

Farmer's Love Letter

By Marge Wenzel, Kent, Illinois

Dearest Susie:

I want you to know my heart (beets) only for you. If you (carrot) all for me, why not ask your parents if they will (lettuce) get married. Since we (cantaloupe), I suppose you will want a big church wedding. Everyone knows I'm (plum) daffy about you, and I'm sure we would make a happy (pear). Please do not (squash) my hopes, because it is love like I have for you that makes a (mango) crazy. You've been the (apple) of my eye for so long, and my love for you is as strong as an (onion). I trust you will never (turnip) your nose at me. If you do, there is only one thing for me to do: I'll go to the river (endive) in.

All my love,
Joe

Double Meanings

By Erma Reynolds, Longmeadow, Massachusetts

GIVE EACH player a pencil and paper listing the following cooking terms. Have them match the word or description "matching" it in the opposite column. Each cooking term has another meaning, and that's the object of the game—to match them. For example, poach means to capture wild game illegally. Allow a few minutes for the game. The person with the most correct wins.

1. stew	share of the loot
2. roast	politician
3. grind	worry
4. baste	dollar bill
5. soak	poke fun at
6. broil	sew with long stitches
7. whip	very diligent student
8. stir	free-for-all
9. bone	overcharge
10. slice	prison

Answers: 1-worry; 2-poke fun at; 3-very diligent student; 4-sew with very long stitches; 5-overcharge; 6-free-for-all; 7-politician; 8-prison; 9-dollar bill; 10-share of the loot.

The Spice of Life

By Mildred Grenier, St. Joseph, Missouri

FILL SMALL paper cups with small amounts of various kitchen spices, such as cinnamon, allspice, cloves, pepper, etc. Number the cups and keep the names of the spices on a piece of paper, for your identification.

Pass the cups around and have each guest smell the contents, then write down what spice she thinks it is. The one who correctly identifies the greatest number of spices is the winner.

Gift Ideas

Apron and Matching Pot Holder Set

**A lovely gift for the bride-to-be.
See both on opposite page.**

Apron

By Jo Wenzel, Kent, Illinois

Materials:
1 yard of 45-inch linen, denim or other heavy
  cotton fabric
bias seam tape
fabric paints
calico fabric scraps

PURCHASE 1 yard of 45-inch wide linen, denim
or some other heavy cotton fabric (This piece is big
enough to make two aprons—so make yourself one
at the same time!)

Cut the fabric into a rectangle measuring 22 x 33
inches. (Save all the scraps.) Measure up from the
bottom (as shown) 21½ inches.

Measure 5½ inches on either side of the middle
fold. (This gives a top width of about 11 inches at
the neckline.) Draw in underarm curves by con-
necting points. Put in seam finishes by turning the
sides under and stitching.

Hem the top of the apron with a 1½-inch fold.
Hem the bottom of the apron with 3-4-inch hem,
depending on the height of the person the apron is
being made for.

Using the long fabric strip scraps, make a neck
piece approximately 23 inches long. Be sure to
"finish" the edges. Add side ties of purchased tape
or make your own.

Chicken Applique
Using the pattern on page 96, carefully sketch the
outline of the chicken on the center top of the

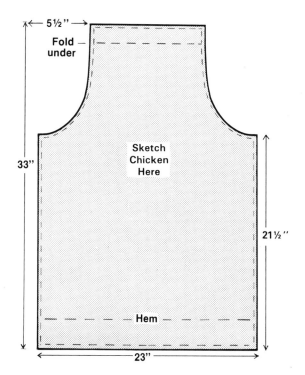

apron. Use fabric paints to color in the body, beak,
comb and eye. While the paint is drying, cut out
wing and tail feathers from a contrasting calico
fabric. Use a zigzag stitch to applique in place.

Potholder

FROM THE remaining apron fabric scraps and
contrasting calico, cut the pieces for this "square
within a square" design. (See pattern on page 95.)
Cut a 9½-inch square of batting (use terry cloth or
fiberfill). Cut a 9½-inch square of fabric for the
backing. Stitch the potholder together by hand or
machine. Edge with bias tape to complete.

Bride's Tool Kit

DECORATE a small tool chest with adhesive
flowers (use your imagination!). Fill with small
tools the new bride will be glad she has around the
house when she's got a small repair to make or a
picture to hang. Some items you could include are:
Screwdriver, pliers, hammer, nails, picture hooks,
tacks, masking tape.

And don't forget a padlock so she can be sure
her *own* tools will always be there when she needs
them! *—Entries too numerous to mention*

A "Welcome" Book

By Mrs. William J. Schmidt, Randolph, Wisconsin

A GREAT GIFT to make a new daughter-in-law or
sister-in-law feel welcome into her new family is a
birthday/address book filled with the addresses,
telephone numbers and birth dates of family
members. It's a nice gesture to say "welcome" and
it's a lasting remembrance.

Dinner Table Pizzazz

With all the colorful, attractive varieties of bed sheets on the market today, it's a shame to keep them exclusively in the bedroom!

By Mary Jane Lamphier, Arlington, Iowa

Materials:
One full-sized bed sheet, 81 x 96 inches
15 yards of wide, color-coordinated rickrack (to match sheet)
yardstick
scissors
thread
interlining or thin batting for place mats

HERE'S A way to create a beautiful tablecloth, napkins and place mats for the new bride—all using a single full-sized sheet. Fold the sheet in half the long way. Cut as shown at right. (This will give you pieces for a 60 x 60-inch tablecloth, six napkins and four place mats.) Do not use hemmed areas of sheet.

Turn under the edge of the tablecloth twice. Press.

Pin rickrack on the wrong side so that half of it extends over on the right side. Stitch the rickrack in place and then stitch around the entire tablecloth again to make sure the hem is secure and both edges of the rickrack are tacked down.

Hem the napkins with a narrow hem, without trim. *(If you want to add trim, you will need eight extra yards of rickrack.)* Use leftover rickrack for a napkin ring, tacking the ends of a 6-inch piece together. Fold the napkin to slip it through the ring.

Cut an interlining for the place mat. Stitch rickrack in place on the right side edge of the place mat.

Make a layer of three: First the interlining, then the back of the mat (wrong side to interlining), then the right side of mat top to right side of mat back. Pin all in place.

Sew together on the stitching line used for sewing down the rickrack. Leave a few inches open on one end so that it can be turned right side out.

Trim seam allowance and corners and turn.

Slip stitch the opening. Press.

Quilt the layers together with the sewing machine. Stitch diagonally, each row two inches apart. Do this in a crisscross pattern.

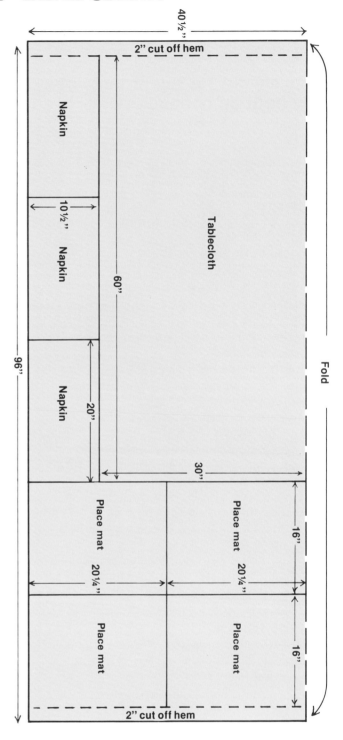

Mystery Cans

By Margaret Penfold, Corning, Iowa

HAVE YOUR guests each bring a can of food with the label removed. Give them to the bride. Many brides have said they would later open a can in the morning and "build it into the day's meals." A fun reminder of the shower for later!

Wedding Invitation Candle

Light up her day with this special wedding momento.

By Mrs. Louis A. Danner, Atalissa, Iowa

IF YOUR bridal shower is a month or less before the "big day" why not put your invitation to the wedding to good use?

Carefully burn an edge around the "message" part of the invitation and glue it onto the candle with "mod-podge" or some other type of combination glue/decoupage substance. Allow to dry thoroughly.

Sponge or brush on, another five to six coats of "mod-podge" over the invitation and the surrounding area, making sure you go over the edges of the invitation well. The glue will dry clear, so it isn't necessary to be real careful about making neat outer edges.

If you have pictures that would look nice with the invitation, affix them on the opposite side of the candle, using the same method.

A Pantry Plus

By Mrs. George Miller, Solon, Iowa

PURCHASE a nice cork-framed bulletin board, colored index cards and push pins. In the weeks before the shower, while you're shopping for your own groceries, purchase "extras" for the new couple.

Write the names of the items you have purchased and stored away on the index cards. Wrap the board, and on the outside make the notation that "the items on this 'grocery list' of cards are waiting at my house for you." It's a very much appreciated gift for a couple starting out. And you can deliver the gift when they get in their new home.

Personalized Dish Towels

By Mrs. Hilbert Gerdes, Goodhue, Minnesota

PASS OUT two or three nice fabric dish towels to your shower guests, and ask them to write their name on the towels somewhere. Then pass out needle and embroidery floss and each guest can embroider hers on while the shower is in progress.

Or, as hostess, take the embroidery portion of the project on yourself, and present the towels to the bride-to-be later on.

Bread Board Momento

By Margaret Penfold, Corning, Iowa

BUY OR make an attractive bread board with a loop at the top for hanging. At the top of the board, attach a photo of the bride and bridegroom opening gifts at a decorated table.

At the shower, have the guests sign their names in the middle of the board. At the bottom, sign your name (as hostess) or attach a photo of yourself. Decoupage the board and give it to the bride.

A rolling pin works well, too!

Recipe Card File

By Julie Fritts, Aldie, Virginia

MAKE OR purchase a nice wooden index card file box, and glue colorful rickrack around the top and bottom edges. On the front, attach a colorful applique, or decoupage a cutout from a magazine. Buy dividers and put them inside with plenty of blank recipe cards.

As the guests arrive, collect their recipe cards (which you sent out with the invitations) and place them in the box. Put the box on the bride's chair.

Bride's Hanger

A momento the bride-to-be will really appreciate—it's perfect to hang her wedding dress on.

By Roylinda Rumbaugh, Mattawan, Michigan

SCRAPS OF any nice dressy, white fabric are fine, and the more trims and laces you can add to make the hanger extra special, the better. (If the bride is making her own dress, scraps of that would be especially nice.) Give a set of two hangers!

Materials:
wooden hanger with a single wooden arm
polyester batting
dressy white fabric (crepe, brocade, crepe de Chine, etc.)
fabric glue
1/2 yard of ribbon
lace to trim

Cut two strips (16- x 2-inch) of batting. Fold lengthwise in half, insert hanger between and glue in several spots to hold.

Cut a bias piece of fabric 1- x 6-inch. Stitch 1/4-inch seam on one end and 1/4-inch seam up the side. Slip over the hanger hook and glue neatly at the bottom.

Cut two 3- x 14-inch fabric strips. Cut two 2-1/2- x 8-1/2-inch fabric strips. Run a gathering thread along the 14-inch sides. Draw up to fit 8-1/2-inch sides of the other pieces. Place right sides together.

Stitch one end, and both sides. Repeat for other pieces. Turn right side out. Slip on hanger. The two pieces will just meet in the center. Tack them down or put a little glue on that spot.

Make sure the gathered part is on top of the hanger. Wrap ribbon twice around the center seam and tie a bow. Add lace where desired, or leave plain.

Perfect Match Gift Cards

By Esther Fahning, Wells, Minnesota

ATTACH a tiny sprig of dried flowers to an ordinary wooden kitchen match, and mount on a plain white gift card.

Attach the card to your wrapped gift, and write on the card "For a couple we think a perfect match."

Cents and Spice

By Mrs. Elroy Jensen, Canby, Minnesota

TYPE UP pages of recipes and put in a folder which has pockets and metal filing tabs. Put "cents off" coupons and other recipes in the pockets. Pack a box of assorted spices to go with this little booklet.

Wedding Shower Corsage

By Mrs. Loren Trunk, Princeton, Minnesota

Materials:
1 8- x 10-inch double thickness green net
1 pair panties
sprigs of artificial leaves and flowers
1 yard ribbon
a cardboard base (green)

GATHER NET with long stitches on the long side. Place green leaves and a spray of flowers onto net.

Gather pantie top in a circle then fold leg lace or elastic around top to form a rose. Sew through with matching thread to hold in place.

Wire them to the top of net and flowers, add ribbon and anchor to a cardboard base.

New Pantsuit for the Bride

Add a smile to her cleaning.

By Mrs. Rodney Voelker, Brownsdale, Minnesota

**"We look like a pantsuit but really we're not.
We are three little Handiwipes—you'll like us
a lot. So take us apart; it really won't hurt.
Then use us for dishes and chasing the dirt."**

Materials:
3 Handiwipes
3 buttons
thread and needle

TAKE ONE Handiwipe and fold it in half with the shorter sides meeting to make the jacket.

Then fold the sides of jacket so they meet in the middle. Fold back a triangular collar on each side. Sew three buttons down the front. Take another Handiwipe and fold in the two long sides so they meet in the middle, and then fold in half. Fold back about 1/2 inch for cuff on each end.

If the sleeve is too wide for a jacket, fold down 1/2 inch or so on the top.

Take the third Handiwipe to form the pants. First fold up about 1/2 inch on the bottom to form the cuffs. Fold up about 1 inch on each side and then fold over so they meet in the middle. Iron over each

piece. Lay the sleeves across the top of the pants and then the jacket on top of that and fasten together with thread and buttons. Attach the verse shown above at left.

The Handy Doll

By Mrs. Rodney Voelker, Brownsdale, Minnesota

Materials:

can of furniture polish	safety pins
wooden spoon	pastry brush
3 dishcloths	paper
rubber band or string	scrub pad
chenille pipe cleaners	1/2-cup measuring
plastic measuring spoons	cup

TAPE a scrub pad to the top of the furniture polish can. Cut a piece of paper to fit spoon back and draw on face. Tape to back of spoon; position spoon on can vertically. Put a 1/2-cup measuring cup on top of the pad. Wrap dishcloths around body, fasten with rubber bands and pins. Fasten a set of small plastic measuring spoons to one arm and a pastry brush to the other, using pipe cleaners.

Crazy Quilt Place Mats

These attractive and cheerful place mats can be made with leftover fabric.

By Mary Allen, Plymouth, New Hampshire

CUT A piece of fabric (light batting or lining) the size you want your place mat to be. (A finished measurement of 17 x 14 inches is good.)

Take pieces of fabric, and starting with one corner of the inside piece, pin a piece of fabric in place. Then lay another piece down, overlapping this over the first piece. Turn the overlapped edge under so no raw edges show.

Keep placing and pinning until the whole backing is covered. Stitch the pieces down with a zigzag stitch. Or, sew in place by hand, first basting the pieces in place. Use a feather stitch or another decorative stitch. Press.

Cut a backing piece the same size as the front.

Baste the two pieces together, wrong sides facing each other. Finish the edges with bias tape and a zigzag (or decorative hand) stitch.

Kitchen Cornucopia

By Bertha Anderson, Sullivan, Illinois

PERCH AN attractive wicker cornucopia (found at department or hobby stores) on a cookie sheet, and fill it with miscellaneous kitchen items such as a tea strainer, wooden spoons, measuring spoons, a grater, spatula and all sorts of colorful and useful utensils. The bride will appreciate it very much.

Trim your gift with a pretty bow tied around the mouth of the "basket" and insert dried flowers and dried wheat stalks.

Who's Grater?

By Esther Fahning, Wells, Minnesota

A CUTE way to give a grater is to wrap it and attach a note reading "You may think (bridegroom's name) is great, but this is a little grater."

Clean Up Time

By Mrs. Elroy Jensen, Canby, Minnesota

PACK A pantry-full of cleaning products for the bride-to-be inside buckets, dish drainers, or vegetable bins.

Green Thumb Gift

By Erma Clevenger, Hamilton, Missouri

IF YOU'D like to inspire a green thumb for the new couple, any or all of the following items would be the perfect shower gift. Fill a wheelbarrow with real or imitation flowers, or simply fill the wheelbarrow with the items suggested below.

Gift Ideas:

plant ties	home soil test kit
potting soil	tomato stakes
almanac	rake
gloves	hoe
hand garden tools	watering can
soaker hose	sprayer
gardening book	compost tablets
wide brimmed hat	plants
canning equipment	pruner

Bountiful Basket

By Estelle Salata, Hamilton, Ontario

DECORATE a wicker laundry basket with streamers and flowers, and fill it with presents for the bride. (You and several of your guests can share this together.) This makes a handy carryall from the shower, and will be put to use for years to come in the bride's new home!

Make Her a Sewing Basket

For every new bride, the days of replacing buttons, mending and "creating" are just about to begin.

By Mary Jane Lamphier, Arlington, Iowa

Materials:
2 5-gallon plastic ice cream containers with wire handles
leather punch
10 yards of plastic craft cord
5 large, 8 small plastic flowers
paper fasteners (1-inch or 1-1/2-inch size)
miscellaneous sewing notions to place in basket when finished

CUT THE bottom out of one pail. Make eight scallops around the bottom of the pail, using the pattern on page 94.

Punch holes, using a leather punch, 1/4-inch from the outer edge of the scallops, every 1/2 inch until all scallops are perforated. Using the pattern on page 94, cut an eight-pointed star from the bottom of the pail you previously cut. Punch holes around the star edges, using the same proportions as the scallops. Edge-lace both the star and scallops with the plastic craft cord. Punch holes around the turned up edge of a pail lid and lace it as well.

Punch a hole about 1 inch below bottom of each scallop, as shown. Make corresponding holes on the other bucket. Place the laced and scalloped pail over the second pail, with the scallops toward the top. Snap on the laced lid to the lip of the laced and scalloped pail. This will hold it in place.

Fasten the inner bucket, the outer scalloped pail and the smaller plastic flowers with paper fasteners. (Do this by poking the fastener through the center of each flower, and on through the corresponding holes in both pails.) Add a few leaves for added interest, if desired.

Punch holes in the second lid and lace it. Place

the laced star in the center of the lid. Using a paper fastener, attach a large flower (or combine the petals of several to make a different flower) in the center. Add four small flowers—one on every other star point. Wrap the wire handle with plastic cord and tie.

Fill the basket with scissors, thread, needles, pins and other sewing notions.

Gifts for Everybody

By Dorothy Patten, Janesville, Iowa

IF YOU'VE been to the kind of bridal shower where it seems like the bride-to-be will never finish opening her gifts, here's a solution that gets everyone involved and makes the gift time go faster.

Have each guest select a gift from the gift table, making sure they don't take the one they brought.

In turns, have each introduce herself, and then open the gift. (If the bride's mother is present, she should start.)

Each guest should tell who the gift is from, and make sure everyone can see it. This method almost always leaves plenty of gifts for the bride to open herself, and everyone feels more a part of that portion of the shower.

Button-On Hand Towels

So handy around the house!

By Marie Hellinger, Shelby, Montana

Materials:
1 hand-size kitchen or bathroom terry towel
coordinating yarn (4 ply gives more body)
1 sharp-headed steel crochet hook—size 8
1 steel crochet hook—size 0
1 large button
   (See page 2 for crochet abbreviations.)

CUT TOWEL in half width-wise. Overcast cut edge on sewing machine. Using the sharp-headed steel hook, sl st about 64 sts evenly across the cut end of the towel.

   Row 1: Switch to larger hook and ch 3; dc in every sl st across.

   Row 2: Ch 3; dc in every *other* dc across.

   Rows 3 and 4: Rep as for row 2, adjusting as needed until there are at least 6 (or another even number more) of dc sts left. Work these remaining sts for about 8 rows, depending on how long you want the towel loop to be.

   Last row: Ch 1, sc 1, dc 1, ch 1, dc 1, sc 1, sl st 1. Break off yarn. There will be a space for button to go through the middle dc sts. Sew button in place.

Patchwork Hostess Apron

By Mary Allen, Plymouth, New Hampshire

USE 7-inch squares of fabric in whatever colors you desire.

   Sew the squares together, using a 3/8-inch seam allowance. Sew five together across for width and six down for length. Press the apron top.

   Take another 7-inch square. Turn under the edges and trim to make a pocket. Use ruffled eyelet lace or rickrack for trim. Then attach the pocket to the apron top with topstitching.

   Place the pressed top on another piece of pressed fabric and cut out a lining the same size as the patchwork top. (Use a pastel or plain fabric for this.)

   Pin, with right sides together. Stitch front and lining together on both sides and bottom, using 3/8-inch seams. Turn and press. Topstitch around sides and bottom, if desired.

   Then pin the tops of front and lining together. Stitch with a gathering stitch. Gather gently and add waistband and ties, as with any gathered apron. Or, use fold-over braid for band and ties.

   For additional trim, you can add ruffled eyelet or rickrack to bottom and sides of apron.

Towel Wedding Cake

By Maria Hellinger, Shelby, Montana

Materials:

1 washcloth	thread
rickrack in several colors	artificial flowers
pins	

2 large solid-color bath towels (3 for 2-tiered cake)

FOLD TOWELS in fifths lengthwise and roll them end to end into a circle. Use another towel if a second tier is needed. Secure with pins or stitch to hold in place. Grasp center of washcloth and flare corners, tucking into center of cake. Decorate with flowers and rickrack to resemble fancy wedding cake.

Picnic Plus

By Mrs. Elroy Jensen, Canby, Minnesota

GIVE a vegetable bin full of paper plates, napkins, foil, plastic wrap, sandwich bags, wax paper, paper cups and other goodies for packing lunches and picnics.

A What's-It-Box

Wrap your gifts creatively!

By Charlotte Roach, Faucett, Missouri

PURCHASE measuring cups and spoons, a flour sifter, a dish mop, a can opener, spoon rest and a mat for hot dishes. Wrap in paper, or use a large bath towel. Fashion on a bow of ribbon and wind around package and a large cooking spoon and two spatulas (one with a long handle and one with a short handle). Attach a card on top which reads:

"This package is called a what's-it-box,
Filled with practical things for you.
A lot of different thing-a-ma-bobs
For jobs all wives must do."

Bride's Scrapbook

By Mrs. Herbert Gerdes, Goodhue, Minnesota

ONE ACTIVITY that's fun at a bridal shower is to have the guests spend a few minutes making a scrapbook for the new couple—either humorous, beautiful, or serious.

Give each guest a blank page from a scrapbook, titled with such things as *Our First Date, We're Engaged!, The Wedding, Our First Home, Our First Meal, Our Honeymoon,* and so on through *Our Golden Anniversary.* Pass out old magazines, scissors, paste and let each guest illustrate or border her page for your guest of honor. Clever or funny, the bride will have a nice momento to take home.

Kitchen Verse Utensils

By Charlotte Roach, Faucett, Missouri

ONE CHARMING way to give some useful kitchen utensils to the bride-to-be is by wrapping them and attaching this verse:

"A rubber scraper for bowls and pans
Thick hot pads to protect your hands.

A dish for butter, a cutlery tray
Some rags for dusting on cleaning day.

A choice of aprons for you to wear
When you're alone, or guests are there.

A small hand towel, adorned with flowers,
Recipes to try for dinner hours."

Wedding Bell Ornament

By Mrs. Louis A. Danner, Atalissa, Iowa

BUY A small Styrofoam or plastic bell. Tear the top layer from the bride and bridegroom's printed napkins (the kind with their name and wedding date on the front) and cut around the names and date and any other decorations on the napkin. Coat with "mod-podge" (or some other brand of combination glue/decoupage substance), and attach the cut out writing. Sprinkle glittery diamond dust (available at craft shops) and allow to dry. Trim with a bead for a clapper. Tie a pretty ribbon on top.

Make several and attach them to a spray-painted twig, if desired.

Design a Cookbook

By Estelle Salata, Hamilton, Ontario

WHY NOT design a cookbook for the bride? Buy a photograph album. Ask each person to bring along a favorite recipe and a photograph of herself. Or, take Polaroid shots of each. Each guest can paste in a photograph of herself, and her favorite recipe beneath it.

An ideal cookbook cover is gingham, pre-pasted wallpaper, self-adhesive decorative vinyl covering, or plastic. Replace the picture album laces with ribbon ties. Paste a heart-shaped photograph of the bride and groom on the cover.

Forever Ribbon Bouquet

Something for the shower!

By Jo Daggett, Maroa, Illinois

BECAUSE it's considered good luck to carry one's shower gift bows during the wedding rehearsal, a handmade bow keeper is a nice gift for the bride-to-be on the day of the shower.

Cut a newspaper heart measuring 15 inches from top to tip. Using that as a pattern, cut two hearts from some net, and sew them together. Trim the edge with a ruffle made of the same net or a contrasting color of net; or use lace. Add a loop of ribbon at the top on the back so the bride can store the heart by hanging it.

Now cut a 4-inch slash *in the back heart only,* being careful not to cut the front heart. If you'd like, add a bow or flower to the front of the heart.

The new bride will enjoy this heart and her shower helper will be able to arrange the bows and ribbons attractively inside the heart through the slit in the back.

Molly the Maid

By Laurie Norris, Hesperia, Michigan

Materials:
1 10-quart pail or a large wastebasket
1 string mop or dust mop
1 circle of cardboard the size of the top of the pail or wastebasket
1 wig stand
2 bath towels
2 hand towels
2 oven mitts
1 apron
2 coat hangers
cleaning supplies (to put in bottom of the pail for weight. Use as many items as you want.)
    window cleaner
    Spic & Span
    scouring powder
    dish soap
2 rubber bottle tops (from soft drinks)
kitchen utensils (use as many as you like)
safety pins (assorted sizes)
wire or tape
crayons or paint
hairpins

PLACE CLEANING supplies in the pail or wastebasket. Fill with newspaper wadded up.

Place cardboard circle in pail. (Make hole in center of cardboard circle and insert mop handle through it, placing handle of mop up.)

Make sure mop is held securely in an upright position, having head removed.

Using crayons or paints, make features (eyes, eyebrows, mouth, nose, etc.) on the wig holder. Place mop head on top of wig holder to be used as hair. Secure with hairpins stuck into Styrofoam wig holder. Place bottle tops on earlobes for earrings with hairpins. Place wig holder (head) on mop handle.

Take coat hangers and straighten them leaving hook on one end and a loop on the other. Attach hook end to the mop handle and secure just below neck with wire and/or tape. Take bath towels, holding ends, and secure at the shoulder seams with pins, allowing them to hang over pail as a dress. Pin short end of hand towels to shoulder seam and cover the coat hangers to make the arms.

On each hand, place an oven mitt, securing with safety pins. Hang the apron around the waist, attaching with safety pins. Using pins, attach various utensils to the apron and on her dress.

Ragbag Windfall

By Evelyn Tuller, Elwood, Kansas

IT TAKES a heap of livin' before the rags necessary for cleaning jobs around the house are accumulated and a new bride is apt to be short of a supply.

A clever shower gift to take up this slack is a cute drawstring ragbag made out of any type of fabric. Nylon net may be used, decorated with felt cutouts, sequins or your own individual touch of decoration, and then filled with a nice collection of useful rags.

If you want to give a little more luxurious variation of this practical gift, stuff a pair of fancy pillowcases with the collection of rags to resemble pillows and pack in a large box covered with net.

Nonsense Gift Tags

Compose your own fun!

By Estelle Salata, Hamilton, Ontario

CUT TAGS into shapes like rolling pins, oven mitts, pots and pans and other utensils. Print these little verses on the appropriate forms, using a felt tip marker. Attach to your gift(s).

Mitt Wit
Some girls get burned and call it quits.
They forget to wear oven mitts!

Pot Lick
Grooms will forget to quarrel and bicker
If they're your number one pot-licker.

Pin Boys
(Attach to a rolling pin)
Maggie once used this on Jiggs
Before the days of Bobby Riggs.

These tags could serve as an entertaining ice-breaker if the guests help to compose other gift tag poems at the shower before the bride arrives. Have each read her "poem" aloud.

Handy Corsage

By Janelle Betts, Waterloo, Iowa

Materials:
mouse trap
measuring spoons (use bright colors!)
plastic net pan scrub pad
a round, metal scrub sponge
small useful tools (screwdriver, etc.)
diaper pin

COLLECT ALL of your corsage materials. Try to use the wedding colors. Choose ribbon that will coordinate with your selection of items.

A large-eyed needle will help gather the open netting with ease. Use the netting as fullness and spread the measuring spoons out as you would a bouquet of flowers. Use the metal scrub sponge as a firm center that other small items can be tied or sewn to. A diaper pin can then be used for the fastener.

You might want to have the corsage be symbolic of the bride or fiance's career. Example: A doctor's surgical glove could be blown up in the fingers and miniature medical tools attached to each finger with bows for a young physician.

Recipe Topper

By Esther Fahning, Wells, Minnesota

INSTEAD of attaching a gift tag or card to your bridal shower gift, attach a recipe card. On one side paste a picture of a little house with flowers around it (or something pretty) and beside the picture, write the bride's name. On the reverse side, write your favorite recipe to share with her.

Give "An Organizer"

By Evelyn Tuller, Elwood, Kansas

A DIFFERENT gift for a shower is a two-drawer file cabinet. Select the pressed board or steel variety, and cover or paint it. Or, leave that task for the couple to do together. Add file folders, separators, a household care guide and a budget book.

For a complimenting shower gift, wrap up "an organization package"—an accordian file, an address book with family members' names, addresses, birthdays and anniversaries, a day-by-day appointment book and a reminder pad.

"Something Special" Linens

By Evelyn Tuller, Elwood, Kansas

IF YOU are handy at sewing, delight your favorite bride with a personalized gift. Choose a pair of printed pillowcases, and buy an extra twin-sized sheet to make a matching nightgown for a "something special" touch.

Personalized Tablecloth

By Margaret Penfold, Corning, Iowa

FOR A bridal shower, have each guest sign a card table sized tablecloth with a fabric pen—each should put on her signature. Reserve the center for the bride's name, the date of the shower and the hostess's name. At the end of the shower, present the informal tablecloth as a momento. Good for baby showers too!

Shower-Perfect Recipes

Refreshing punch, tasty sweets and clever serving ideas make any shower or gathering of friends a memorable occasion!

Golden Sherbet Punch

By Mrs. Robert Towne, Tekoa, Washington

    2 cups sugar
    14 small sprigs fresh mint leaves
    2 cups boiling water
    1/4 cup lemon juice
    1 12-ounce can apricot nectar, chilled
    1 6-ounce can frozen concentrate for
        limeade, defrosted
    1 6-ounce can frozen concentrate for orange
        juice, defrosted
    1 6-ounce can frozen concentrate for
        pineapple juice, defrosted
    2 1-quart bottles ginger ale, chilled
    1 quart lemon sherbet

COMBINE SUGAR, mint and boiling water. Stir until sugar is dissolved. Cool; chill. Strain into chilled punch bowl. Add lemon juice, apricot nectar and juice concentrates, mixing well. Carefully pour in ginger ale. Top with small scoops of sherbet; garnish with fresh mint sprigs. (If desired, pineapple, orange or lime sherbet may be used.) Yield: 20 to 25 servings.

Banana Punch

By Mrs. Herb Smith, Colbert, Washington

4 cups sugar
6 cups water
1 6-ounce can frozen concentrate for lemonade
1 6-ounce can frozen concentrate for orange juice
1 quart pineapple juice
5 bananas, mashed
2 quarts clear carbonated beverage, chilled

COMBINE SUGAR and water; bring to a boil, stirring constantly. Remove from heat; add remaining ingredients except carbonated beverage. Pour into freezer trays; freeze until slushy. To serve, fill an 8 or 10-ounce glass half full with frozen mixture; finish filling glass with carbonated beverage. Stir gently to mix. Yield: 15 to 18 servings.

Mrs. Haire's Party Punch

By Mrs. Leslie Conn, Thawville, Illinois

    1 46-ounce can grapefruit juice
    2 46-ounce cans orange juice
    2 46-ounce cans grapefruit-orange juice
    2 46-ounce cans pineapple juice
    1/4 cup lemon juice
    3 packages (0.14-oz. size) raspberry-flavored
        instant soft drink mix (Kool-Aid)
    3 cups sugar
    6 quarts cold water
    2 quarts sweetened, medium-strength tea
    6 1-quart bottles ginger ale

COMBINE FIRST nine ingredients in very large container. At serving time, add ginger ale. (Add 1 quart ginger ale to each 3 quarts of fruit juice mixture.) Add ice to punch bowl. Yield: 125 to 130 servings.

Baby Bottle Punch

By Beth Tobler, Appleton, Wisconsin

A UNIQUE way to serve punch at a baby shower is to use baby bottles. Glass bottles are best for this.

Tie a bow at the neck of the bottle with ribbon that contrasts with the color of the punch. (Do not use the nipples or tops of the bottles.) Fill with punch and serve with a straw. It will add a festive and interesting touch to any baby shower.

Country Theme Goodies

By Mrs. Harold Leisinger, Summer, Iowa

SERVE LEMONADE from a large crock, jug or some other "traditional" country antique, and use an old, decorative ladle.

Serve colorful and tasty cheeses, cut in little cubes, fruit cups and crackers, and a variety of dips. Make a calico chicken for a centerpiece, and place it on a nest of straw with real eggs.

Place a little ivy plant in an old-fashioned pint jar next to the chicken, and place the latest issue of the bride's favorite magazine *(Farm Wife News?)* alongside, with a card saying the shower guests have given her a subscription.

Perfect Sweetheart Cookies

By Mildred Grenier, St. Joseph, Missouri

MAKE YOUR favorite rolled cookie dough. Cut half of it with round cookie cutters and half with scalloped cutters. In the center of each scalloped cookie cut out a small heart with a cookie cutter or sharp knife. Spread the round cookie with a red jam or jelly, top with the scalloped cookie, and bake as usual.

Rainbow Ice Cream Cake

By Mrs. Frank DeHaas, Greencreek, Idaho

1 10-inch round angel food cake, baked
1 3-ounce package each, of strawberry, lime and orange gelatin
1 10-ounce package frozen, sliced strawberries, partly thawed
1/2 gallon vanilla ice cream, slightly softened
1 20-ounce can crushed pineapple, drained
1 11-ounce can of mandarin orange slices, drained

TEAR CAKE into small pieces. Divide into thirds; place in medium bowls. Sprinkle strawberry gelatin over one bowl of cake pieces, lime over the second and orange over the third. Toss each lightly with a fork until cake is well coated with gelatin. Place strawberry cake pieces in bottom of a 10-inch tube pan. Sprinkle any excess gelatin over cake. Spoon strawberries over cake; spread 1/3 of ice cream over strawberries.

Repeat layers with lime cake pieces, pineapple, ice cream; orange cake pieces, oranges and ice cream. Freeze until firm. Unmold on a chilled dessert plate. Slice to serve.

Candy Strawberries

By Mrs. Francis Snow, Mill Run, Pennsylvania

2 3-ounce packages strawberry gelatin
1 cup ground pecans
3/4 cup condensed milk
1 cup flaked coconut
1/2 teaspoon vanilla
red decorator's sugar

COMBINE GELATIN, pecans and coconut. Stir in milk and vanilla, mix well. Chill one hour. Shape into strawberries. Roll in red sugar. Insert paper leaves into top of berry.

You can also make oranges or lemons by using orange or lemon gelatin and orange or yellow decorator's sugar.

Rhubarb Torte

By Mrs. Rodney Voelker, Brownsdale, Minnesota

2 cups flour
1/2 teaspoon salt
3/4 cup brown sugar, packed
3/4 cup butter or shortening
2 cups oatmeal
6 cups fresh rhubarb, cut into 1-inch segments
8 eggs
Dash of salt
3 cups sugar
1/2 cup flour
Cinnamon

MIX TOGETHER with pie blender, flour, salt, brown sugar, butter and oatmeal. Line a 10 x 14-inch pan with all but 1 cup of the mixture, pressing it down firmly.

Spread rhubarb over crust. Beat together the eggs, salt, sugar and flour; pour over rhubarb. Sprinkle remaining oatmeal mixture over top. Sprinkle top of torte lightly with cinnamon. Bake at 350° 1 hour or until custard is done. (Knife inserted in center should come out clean.)

Strawberry Dessert

By Mrs. Frank DeHaas, Greencreek, Idaho

1 10-ounce package of frozen strawberries, thawed
18-20 large marshmallows or 1-1/2 cups of miniature marshmallows
1/2 cup butter
1 cup flour
1/4 cup brown sugar, packed
1/2 cup nuts (optional)
1/2 pint heavy cream, whipped

DRAIN STRAWBERRIES, reserve juice. Melt marshmallows in top of double boiler with juice of strawberries. When melted, cool. While this cools, mix together the butter, flour, brown sugar and nuts. Spread in a 13 x 9-inch pan and bake for 15 minutes at 400°. Remove from oven and stir with a fork to crumble.

Place half of the crumbs in the bottom of a 9 x 9-inch pan. When marshmallow mixture is cool, fold in berries and whipped cream. Sprinkle with remaining crumb mixture; refrigerate several hours.

Mini Cheesecakes

By Carla Read, Henry, Illinois

2 8-ounce packages cream cheese
3/4 cup sugar
2 eggs
1 tablespoon lemon juice
1 teaspoon vanilla
1 small box vanilla wafer cookies
Fruit pie filling
Mini foil baking cups

PLACE A vanilla wafer in the bottom of each mini foil cup. Mix remaining ingredients well (except pie filling) and pour over the wafer, filling 1/2 to 2/3 full. Bake at 375⁰ for 20 minutes. Cool.

Top each cake with 1 tablespoon of pie filling (blueberry, cherry, etc.). These freeze very well so you can make them ahead of time. **Note:** They do *not* store well in the refrigerator, however, as they become soft and mushy after a number of hours. Yield: 12 to 16 servings.

Mint Dazzler

By Mrs. Rodney Voelker, Brownsdale, Minnesota

2 cups vanilla wafer cookie crumbs
1/4 cup melted butter
1/2 cup butter
1-1/2 cup confectioners' sugar
2 eggs, beaten
3 squares chocolate, melted
1-1/2 cups whipped cream
1 8-ounce package of miniature
   marshmallows
1/2 cup crushed peppermint candy

MIX VANILLA cookie crumbs and 1/4 cup melted butter; press into a 13 x 9-inch pan. Cream 1/2 cup butter and confectioners' sugar. Add beaten eggs and melted chocolate; beat until light and fluffy. Spoon over crumbs. Place in freezer while you whip the cream. Fold marshmallows into the whipped cream and spread over the chocolate layer. Sprinkle with candy; refrigerate until serving.

Diaper Tarts

By Ruth Stroh, Cockeysville, Maryland

ROLL out your favorite pie dough recipe. Cut into triangles, and fill with a small amount of a berry pie filling—cherry, apple, blueberry, etc. Lap as you would a diaper. Bake. When slightly cooled, decorate with a tiny icing "pin".

Honeymoon Pie

By Mrs. Rodney Voelker, Brownsdale, Minnesota

43 Ritz crackers, crushed
1/2 cup plus 2 tablespoons of butter, melted
2 packages of instant pistachio pudding
1-1/2 cup milk
1 quart vanilla ice cream, softened
2 Heath candy bars

MIX CRACKER crumbs and melted butter together. Press into 9-inch pie pan; bake at 350⁰ for 10 minutes. Cool.

Beat pudding and milk well. Mix in ice cream. Pour into crust; freeze for 2 hours. Top with whipped cream and sprinkle with crushed candy bars. Return to freezer for another hour.

Cherry Chiffon Pie

By Mrs. Rodney Voelker, Brownsdale, Minnesota

Crust:
1-1/2 cups old fashioned oats, uncooked
1/2 cup chopped nuts
1/2 cup butter, melted
1/4 cup brown sugar, packed

Filling:
1 envelope unflavored gelatin
1/4 cup cold water
1 21-ounce can cherry pie filling
2 egg whites
1/3 cup sugar
1 cup heavy cream, whipped

CRUST: Toast oats and nuts in large shallow baking pan at 350⁰ for about 12 minutes. Combine oats, nuts, butter and brown sugar. Mix well. Press onto bottom and sides of buttered 9-inch pie plate. Chill. FILLING: Soften gelatin in cold water; stir over low heat until dissolved. Place pie filling in blender; cover. Process at "chop" for 5 seconds. Combine cherries and dissolved gelatin in large bowl. Beat egg whites until foamy. Gradually add sugar, beating until stiff peaks form. Fold into cherry mixture. Fold in whipped cream; spoon into crust. Chill about 3 hours or until firm.

Baby Doll Cookies

By Sue Schneck, Racine, Wisconsin

ROLL OUT your favorite sugar cookie dough. Cut out shapes with a gingerbread cookie cutter and bake. Decorate with red cheeks, smiles and tiny frosting diapers. Trim the corners of the diapers with silver candy beads to form diaper pins.

Banana Bread

By Cathy Gondek, San Antonio, Texas

1 cup salad oil
2 cups sugar
4 eggs
2 teaspoons vanilla
4 cups flour
2 cups mashed bananas
6 teaspoons baking powder
1 teaspoon salt
2 cups chopped nuts (optional)

COMBINE ingredients in large mixing bowl; beat until well blended. Bake in 2 large or 4 small greased loaf pans for 1-1/4 hours at 350°.

Easy Baked Alaska

By Cathy Gondek, San Antonio, Texas

1 package white or yellow cake mix
1/2 gallon ice cream, colorful flavor
6 egg whites
12 tablespoons sugar
3 teaspoons cream of tartar

BAKE cake mix in either 13 x 9-inch pan or round layer pans. Place cooled cake(s) on wooden breadboard. Cover top with 1 or 1-1/2 inches of ice cream. (Usually 1/2 gallon will easily cover 2 9-inch rounds.)

Place cake in freezer while you prepare meringue. Beat egg whites until soft peaks form. Gradually sprinkle on cream of tartar and sugar, beating until stiff and glossy. Working quickly, apply meringue to sides first. **Note:** Be sure to have a good thick covering of meringue where cake meets the board to insulate the cake and ice cream from high heat in the oven. A good seal is critical. After sides are covered, spoon remaining meringue on top, forming soft swirls. Carefully place in freezer again.

Just before serving, preheat oven to 450° or 500°, and whisk the Alaska into oven for 3-6 minutes—just until meringue peaks begin to brown. Slice and serve.

Easy Economical Punch

By Virginia Kaska, Atalissa, Iowa

3 46-ounce cans of Hi-C fruit drink
3 packages of pre-sweetened Kool-Aid
4-1/2 quarts of water
3 large bottles of 7-Up

USE flavors that will make the color you want. Mix together, chill and serve. Yield: 36 cups.

Trimming Ideas

By Mrs. Elroy Jensen, Canby, Minnesota

THERE are endless possibilities for decorating your shower goodies—just take a stroll through the novelty section of a dime store sometime, and see all the baby rattles, buggies, wee baby dolls and cribs there. Atop your favorite colorful frosting, you can't lose!

Baby Cupcakes

By Ruth Stroh, Cockeysville, Maryland

FROST your baby shower cupcakes with pastel pinks, blue, green or yellow frosting, and decorate with individual letters—B-A-B-Y, etc. or B-O-Y and G-I-R-L.

Dressy Cubes

By Mary E. Allen, Plymouth, New Hampshire

MAKE FANCY ice cubes or ice rings for your punch by freezing chunks of pineapple and maraschino cherries in juice—either as cubes or in a pretty ring mold.

Cake and Sherbet

By Mrs. Rodney Voelker, Brownsdale, Minnesota

ANGEL FOOD cake served with scoops of sherbet (try strawberry, lime, orange, lemon, raspberry, etc.) makes very attractive dessert. Serve punch in matching colors!

Vegetable Dip

By Cathy Gondek, San Antonio, Texas

1 cup salad dressing or mayonnaise
1 cup sour cream
1 tablespoon chopped parsley
*1 teaspoon celery salt
*1/2 teaspoon garlic salt
1 tablespoon lemon juice
1 tablespoon sugar
1/2 teaspoon paprika
*1/4 teaspoon pepper

PREPARE dip at least a few hours before serving. If a zestier dip is desired, increase starred ingredients.

Invitations & Birth Announcements

Kimono Invitation

So delicate and cute!

By Mrs. Frank Dehaas, Greencreek, Idaho

CUT A RECTANGLE 3½ x 6 inches from a piece of paper. Place the pattern along the fold on a piece of baby shower wrapping paper, and cut around the edge. Open the wrapping paper, and fold each outside edge in to meet at the center fold.

One inch from the top on each side, make a 1-inch cut. Fold the paper below the cut toward the center, and glue in place on the back side of the kimono. Fold a lapel back on each side of the top, and glue on scraps of felt. Add a yarn tie to front. (Shown at left.) Write your shower message inside.

Rattle Time!

By Esther Fahning, Wells, Minnesota

USING STIFF white paper, cut a rattle shape, using the pattern shown on page 94. Be sure to place the pattern on a fold. Trim the rattle with scraps of rickrack and felt, and write your message inside.

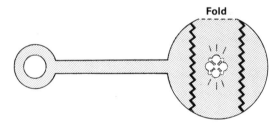

Fold

Diaper Invitations

BUY TINY gift card envelopes. Cut a tiny diaper shape from pastel-colored construction paper, and glue a message-sized rectangle of white paper inside. Write your invitation, fold and pin in the shape of a diaper.

—Entries too numerous to mention

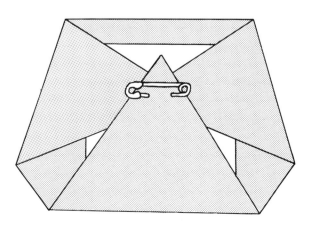

Baby Buggy Invitation

By Beth Tobler, Appleton, Wisconsin

THIS BRIGHT little buggy invitation (opposite) can be made easily with just a paper punch and construction paper. Punch the colors you wish to use. Remove the paper circles from the punch. Glue the circles on the invitation in the shape of a baby buggy. Write your message inside.

Toy Train Invitation

By Jo Wenzel, Kent, Illinois

WHY BUY shower invitations, when you can have so much fun making them yourself!

Cut a rectangle from heavy paper, measuring 8½ x 5¼ inches. Fold widthwise. Using the pattern shown here, cut a train engine from a scrap of calico fabric, and glue in place. Find an interesting circular shape in your fabric scraps, and use it for a rear wheel. Draw in the smokestack, smoke, cowcatcher and front wheels. Your invitation is ready to write and mail! (See photo at left.)

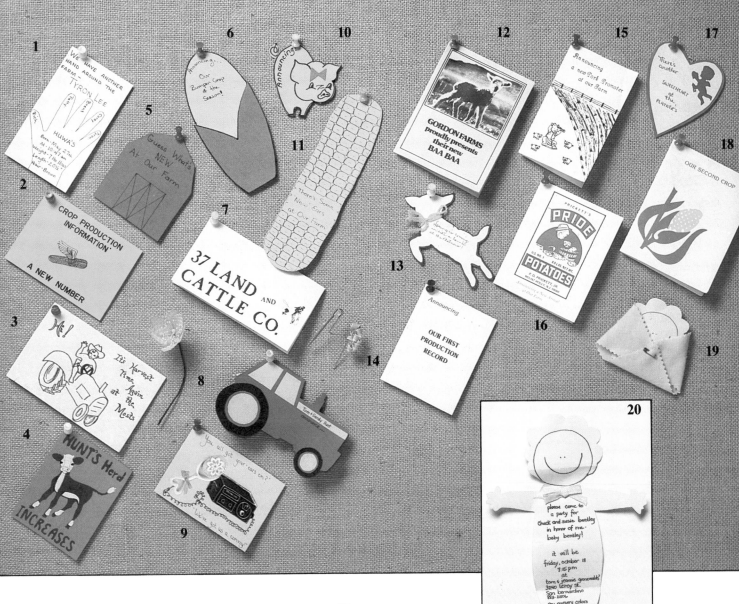

Make Your Own Birth Announcements!

Why buy them when it's so much fun to make them!

WITH NICE PAPER, a little imagination, and excitement over the birth of your child, you can make terrific birth announcements that have a very special meaning for your family! Here's a small sampling of birth announcements, and the stories behind them. The numbers above correspond with the creators of each individual announcement, listed here and on the next few pages.

1 Farm Hand
Without much expense or fuss, Richard and Patty Huwa of Keenesburg, Colorado drew their birth announcements on postcards. Little Tyron (on the pinkie finger) was their newest farm hand!

2 New Crop Information
Because Mark and Joleen Nechanicky of Buckingham, Iowa raise and sell seed corn, centering their birth announcement around seed seemed natural. Inside headings such as variety, maturity date, stalk height and plant appearance were used to describe "female", the birthdate, the baby's length, and hair and eye color!

3 Harvesttime Extra
When Derrick David Most of Crete, Illinois was born, his parents heralded him as an October harvesttime bonus. According to the inside, David was 20% moisture, and "our new alarm clock."

4 Hunt's New Heifer
With bright orange construction paper, and warm brown paints, Russell and Alayne Hunt of Bridgeville, California announced the latest arrival on their cattle ranch. The Hunts called themselves the sire and dam, and even listed "previous calves" Amanda and Jesse as well!

5 Guess What?
David and Kathy Skiba spent the summer prior to their daughter's birth rebuilding a barn they'd lost in a fire. When Kari was born, they held an "open barn" to show off new barn and daughter.

6 Bumper Crop
Allen and Marilyn Platner of Marion, Iowa made this "corny" invitation to announce their new baby's birth.

7 New Board Member
Richard and Sue Waller of Holdrege, Nebraska designed their son's birth announcement on the farm stationery, and named him a new member of the board of directors. His qualifications? He has a way with people, keeps good hours, and for favorite pastimes, drinks and sleeps a lot.

8 Tractor Message
This announcement, patterned after one made by Ted and Jamy Preul of Truxton, Missouri, is made in the shape of a tractor with information about the bumper crop, harvest date, time, and yield. Naturally, the new infant was an "early riser" with "natural drainage."

9 New "Handle" at Home 20!
Randy and LaJeanne Haecker of Plymouth, Nebraska used their enthusiasm for CB lingo in their birth announcement. The 10-36 time, base station, and volume were noted inside with "pride and joy." Even a rattle on the front as a microphone!

10 Cutie Pig!
The same year Bruce and Kathy Thiemke bought their own hog farm, their third child was born. The whole family worked on the announcements together, right down to placing the pink bow!

11 New Ears
What better way for a corn-raising Indiana family to announce their newest arrival than with some "new ears" from their farm? Ike and Mary Beth Brubaker of Huntington, Indiana hand drew each kernel of corn on 55 announcements!

12 New Baa Baa
Dave and Jodie Gordon of Springfield, Ohio raise a variety of crops as well as 150 head of sheep. When their son was born, friends from Texas designed their announcement about their new "baa baa."

13 Spring Lamb
The Platners made another cute birth announcement with this spring lamb. The yarn tie added a nice soft, three-dimensional touch.

14 First Born
For their first child, Steve and Jane Bowen of Caledonia, Michigan designed an official production record for their daughter. Some of the information: "A strong healthy calf with a deep body standing on a good set of legs"; "you'll be hearing more about this stylish young heifer in the future!"

15 New Pork Promoter
"Hope you'll excuse us for making a fuss, but nothing this great ever happened to us!" said the inside of this cute announcement made by Dennis and Jone Molyneux of Rose Hill, Iowa. Their new daughter joined the family pork business as "the prize pork product of the season."

16 Prickett's Potatoes Special
Bushels of love will be spent on the newest arrival at the Phillip Prickett household in Mount Holly, New Jersey.

17 A New Sweetheart
There's a new sweetheart at the Platner place—announced by this cute little heart pasted on a red paper background. A Cupid adds a nice touch.

18 Our Second Crop
Phillip Prickett and his wife silkscreened these beautiful crop birth announcements for the birth of their second daughter..."Heavy Finisher"—7 lbs., 8 ozs. and "Strong Stalk"—21 inches.

19 Baby Bentley Invitation
Jeannie Gronewald of San Bernadino, California made this adorable "pop up" baby shower invitation for a shower she hosted for an expectant friend. She bought pastel-colored envelopes, and made flannel diapers to hold the little "Baby Bentley"...

20 When friends received their shower invitations, "Baby Bentley" popped out to give all the vital shower information. A really cute idea!

Favors, Place Cards & Centerpieces

Bootie Mint Cup

So dainty and cute!

TAKE A small amount of opaque plastic (make sure it's flexible) and cut it into the three pattern pieces shown on page 96. (See upper right on opposite page.)

Punch holes every 3/8 inch around the edge of each piece and crochet together in a pastel-colored fine yarn.

Place a tiny paper mint cup inside, and fill the bootie with mints or nuts and put at each place setting. Or, cut pattern in felt and sew together by hand with colorful yarn.

—Entries too numerous to mention

Felt Bootie Favor

By Eleanor Nolin, Cissna Park, Illinois

USING THE pattern on page 96, cut out pieces of felt. Embroider a pretty toe on the bootie, and stitch the pieces together, using a loose running stitch. (See opposite page, upper left.)

You can put a nut cup inside, or trim packages with this cute shoe on the opposite page!

Paper Bootie Nut Cup

By Mrs. Loren Trunk, Princeton, Minnesota

CUT THE pattern on page 95 in a pretty paper. Punch tiny holes where the laces go in the front of the shoe, and lace with ribbon in an attractive color. Glue or staple the back edges, overlapping them. Place a small paper nut cup inside, as shown opposite. (See bootie on bottom, opposite.)

Lacy Parasol Favors

By Mrs. LaVerne Majerus, Brownsdale, Minnesota

FOLD a 5-6-inch paper doily in half. Cut a semicircle slightly smaller than the folded doily from colored paper. Place inside the doily. (See at right.)

Fold the doily again with the colored paper inside. Glue one end of a pipe cleaner inside the parasol to form a handle. Bend the end of the pipe cleaner for a curved handle, and tie on a tiny ribbon bow to match the color of the colored paper.

"Baby" Flower

By Mrs. R. G. Adams, Valier, Montana

TRIM the center of a fabric flower by buying tiny plastic or rubber babies from a dime store. Place them in the center of the flower petals.

Baby Rattle Favor

By Mrs. Otto Fahning, Wells, Minnesota

DIP A LARGE marshmallow in some very soft frosting. Roll it lightly in a fine, cake decorating candy, and top with chips of hardened marshmallow. Attach a small marshmallow on one side. Insert a pink or blue pipe cleaner for the rattle handle, and place on wax paper until the frosting sets. Tie the handle with a pink or blue bow.

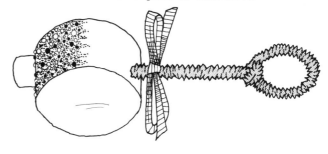

Flower Nut Cup

So easy to make!

By Mrs. LaVerne Majerus, Brownsdale, Minnesota

Materials:
colored construction paper
glue
soda straws (plastic)
small amount of Styrofoam

CUT a flower shape from pastel-colored construction paper, using the pattern given on page 97. Make slits as marked, and lap the paper into a cone shape and glue in place. Cut off a small portion of the cone point big enough to insert a plastic soda straw into the hole. Insert the straw 3 inches into the flower, and stick one end into Styrofoam cut to fit the inside of the nut cup.

Cut leaves of green paper, and insert in Styrofoam at base of straw stem. Fill with nuts or candy to cover Styrofoam. (See nut cup at right.)

Another Bootie Favor

By Mrs. Clifford Johnson, Owatonna, Minnesota

CUT YOUR "bootie" from the bottom of an oval detergent bottle, as shown.

Slit one edge to make a flap for the bootie tongue, and round off the top of the flap. Punch holes down the sides of each bootie, and lace the bootie together with pink or blue ribbon or yarn, pulling the sides over the tongue gently.

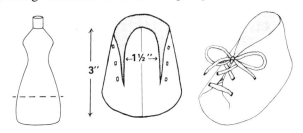

Baby Buggy Nut Cup

By Mrs. Clifford Johnson, Owatonna, Minnesota

BUY some pretty paper nut cups, and cut four paper wheels for each. Add a paper hood the proper size, using the shape shown on page 95.

Attach the hood to the buggy with a pipe cleaner, and then through the sides of the cup, bending the ends to hold the buggy together. Now the pipe cleaner is your buggy handle! (See at right.)

Egg Carton Nut Cups

By Mary Allen, Plymouth, New Hampshire

CUT a Styrofoam egg carton into individual egg-cups. Cut the edge of each in a zigzag line to resemble a broken egg shell. Attach a colored pipe cleaner for a handle, as shown above.

Fill the cups with nuts or mints. Or, to use as a favor, fill with tiny dried flowers.

Cuddle-Up Centerpiece

By Betty Siemers, Grand Island, Nebraska

WRAP A cute stuffed animal in a receiving blanket and place it a cradle on the table for a centerpiece. The new baby can play with it later.

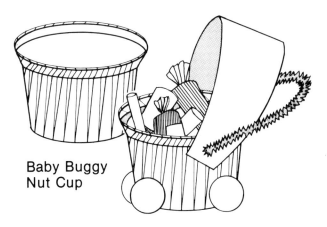

Baby Buggy
Nut Cup

Umbrella Favor

A dainty, pretty favor favorite!

By Ann Brower, Keota, Iowa

Materials:
colorful paper napkins (try an all-over design with border type)
large 3/8-inch chenille stems
1/4 x 20-inch ribbon
invisible scotch tape

LEAVE THE napkin folded in quarters. Line the center corner of the napkin by placing 2-inch strips of scotch tape across the corner to reinforce it.

Cut off a very tiny tip at the center with it folded, then open the napkin and slip a chenille stem through the hole. Be careful not to tear the napkin any more than necessary. Slip the stem through about 1 inch.

Carefully smooth out one short-side fold down along the stem, and secure the bottom edge to the stem with a 2-inch strip of scotch tape. Repeat with the other three short folds on the other sides of the stem. Smooth down each long, diagonal fold along the stem and secure it to the stem with scotch tape.

Finish off the pointed ends of the napkin by wrapping scotch tape around the stem to hold all securely. Flatten the tape wrapping. If necessary, add a tiny gold star seal to each side as a "cover up".

Tie a 10-inch length of ribbon around the scotch-taped stem and tie into a bow. Curve the bottom end of the stem into an umbrella handle. At the top

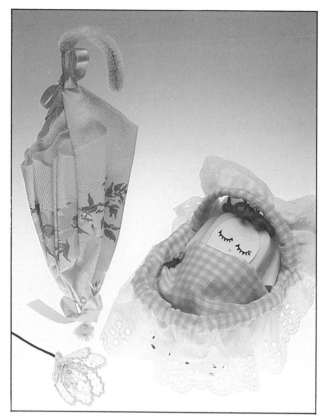

Make some pretty favors for your next baby shower. Directions are on this page and next.

of the umbrella, arrange the folds attractively. Wrap a piece of tape around the top to keep the napkin from slipping. Tie a bow at the top using remaining ribbon. Fold the stem to form a knob.

Dainty Fabric Flowers

By Eleanor Nolin, Cissna Park, Illinois

CUT five or six petals using this pattern from dotted swiss or some other fairly stiff, but sheer fabric. Glue 4 inches of rickrack around each petal, using a complimentary color.

Allow to dry. Purchase some flowers stamens from a craft store (see flower in photo above) and attach at end of a 4-5 inch piece of wire. Hold the petals around the stem and wrap with thread and knot. Wrap the stem in floral tape.

These flowers can be made bigger or smaller.

Soapy Favors

By Roylinda Rumbaugh, Mattawan, Michigan

HERE'S A useful and cute baby shower favor that the mother-to-be can put to use after the party's over. Make several and she'll have a nice supply for her new baby. (See photo above.)

Glue or tape a band of white, black or flesh-colored construction paper around a bar of baby soap. Glue loops of yarn to form hair on the paper, and paint on a cute face. Pin a contrasting-color diaper on the soap and secure with a pin.

Flower Petal
Cut 6

Finished Petal

Baby Basket Centerpiece

Here's a centerpiece idea that the new mother can use later as a planter, letter basket, etc.

(See photo on page 59.)

By Roylinda Rumbaugh, Mattawan, Michigan

Materials:
small oval or rectangular wicker basket, with a handle that can be removed
wide lace or eyelet trim
fiberfill
ribbon
fabric scraps
fabric glue

CAREFULLY remove the handle from the basket. Reattach the handle near one end using a stapler or another workable method. Gather lace or eyelet trim with long, running stitches, and fit around the edge of the basket. Adjust gathers evenly, and slip stitch onto basket over the edge.

Stitch more trim around the basket, attaching the second layer to the first to create a tiered look. Slip stitch two layers of trim on the handle. Using either ribbon or fabric scraps (gingham is nice) cover the handle and rim of the basket. This will hide your stitches. Glue in place.

Make a baby mattress with fiberfill. Make a white sheet and pillow with fabric, and cut a cover with pinking shears. If you are giving the basket after the baby is born, stitch the child's name and birthdate on the cover.

Depending on how large a basket you make, fix a small pot of live or plastic flowers and set inside the baby basket, or give the flowers as a separate gift for the mother to place in the basket later on.

If you've made a fairly large basket, put trial size "pretties" for the mother-to-be inside...special lotions, colognes, shampoos, etc.

Or, fill the basket with baby things like diaper pins, rattles, etc.

A Bootie Tree

By Ruth Stroh, Cockeysville, Maryland

A LOVELY and practical way to trim the table is by placing an attractive branch of a tree in a bowl, anchoring it with clay. (Be sure to take off the leaves.) Have each guest bring a pair of colorful booties, and as the guests arrive, hang them on the branches; or, use lollipops and pacifiers.

Bootie Centerpiece

By Mrs. Clifford Johnson, Owatonna, Minnesota

CUT A bootie from the bottom of a large bleach bottle as shown.

Make two vertical slits to make a flap. This forms bootie tongue. Round off top of flap. Punch holes (as shown) down edges adjacent to tongue. Lace together with pink or blue ribbon or yarn, pulling sides over the tongue.

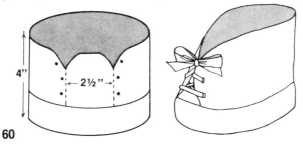

Kimono Napkin

By Mrs. William J. Schmidt, Randolph, Wisconsin

FOR A PRETTY napkin next to your fancy refreshment plates, try a little kimono napkin—made with a couple of folds and two easy cuts.

Take a beverage napkin and unfold once. Fold each half in until they are lined up with the middle fold of the napkin. Two inches from the top of the napkin (the side that is not open) make a 1/2-inch cut on each side as shown.

Turn the edges below the cut to the inside, and form a crease. This makes the sleeve. Now fold back the top corners of the napkin to make tiny lapels!

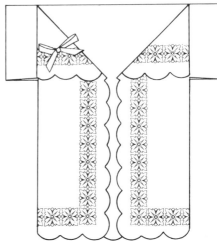

Hat Basket Centerpiece

A neat, simple centerpiece.

By Mrs. Clifford Johnson, Owatonna, Minnesota

CUT OFF the bottom portion of a half gallon bleach bottle, as shown, and glue it to a 12-inch circle of cardboard covered with colored paper.

Clip the edges of this "brim" to look like straw. Add crepe paper or ribbon to form a hat band, and add a bow for decoration. Fill your "hat" with tiny useful gifts such as baby lotion, powder, toys, safety pins, etc.

Flannel Diaper Nut Cups

By Anna Mary Yoder, Middlebury, Indiana

BUY (or use scraps of) pastel-colored flannel fabric. Cut into triangles approximately 7½ x 5½ x 5½ inches.

Dip the pieces of flannel into melted parrafin. Place on wax paper and cool slightly. When cool enough to handle, shape into a diaper and pin together with a small safety pin. Fashion a cup area so the diaper will sit on the table without tipping. When hardened, these make unique mint or nut holders for your shower refreshment table.

Quick and Easy Stork Favor

BEND THE CLASP of a large safety or diaper pin into an S-shape to form stork's neck and head.

Insert a colored cocktail toothpick in the clasp to form the stork's bill. If you use a safety pin, paint the pin and toothpick a matching shade.

For wings, pull a 2-inch bit of ribbon through the hole and flare it out. Or, insert a small triangle of bright construction paper. Tuck the standing leg into a gumdrop, marshmallow, dab of clay, egg carton cup or cupcake. (See left.)

Cut out small diamond-shaped place cards, fold in half, and glue the tips together. Hang from the toothpick "bill". Add names for each guest.

—Entries too numerous to mention

Napkin Diaper Cup

By Mrs. Rodney Voelker, Brownsdale, Minnesota

CUT a diaper shape (triangle) out of a paper beverage or dinner napkin, with an old pair of pinking shears. Fold and fasten with a small safety pin. The cup will stand when filled with nuts or mints.

Oatmeal Box Cradle

By Esther Fahning, Wells, Minnesota

CUT a round oatmeal box into a hooded cradle shape. Trim with pink, white and blue tissue paper, ribbons and flowers.

Use a bottle of baby oil as the mattress, a bar of baby soap for the pillow and buy a rattle (preferably one with a painted face) to lay down inside.

Place Cards

For your fancy shower table!

Shower Place Cards

By Marge Wenzel, Kent, Illinois

THESE attractive place cards take just a minute to make! Cut a 2-3/4 x 3-1/2-inch piece of white poster paper and fold lengthwise. Glue on a brightly-colored piece of felt cut in the shape of an umbrella top. Draw in drops of water, the umbrella handle and the guest's name, as shown at right.

Shower Name Tags

By Marge Wenzel, Kent, Illinois

IF YOU'D like your shower guests to feel at ease, the easy-to-make name tags in the photo at right are perfect.

Cut a 3-1/2 x 3-1/2-inch square of white poster paper. Round the corners. Glue a tiny feather and a pretty button at one side of the card as shown. Draw in a stork, grass, and the "bundle of joy". Write in that guest's first name. Make enough for everyone to wear.

Diaper Place Cards

By Ruth Stroh, Cockeysville, Maryland

USE A tiny cocktail napkin, pinned as a diaper with a tiny safety pin, as a cute place card at your guest's table. Attach the diaper to a toothpick and stick in a cupcake. (See photo below.)

Choo Choo Place Card

By Jo Wenzel, Kent, Illinois

CUT cards from stiff poster paper, measuring 5½ x 3½ inches. Fold in half widthwise. Using the pattern shown here, cut the engine shape in a calico scrap. Using magic markers, draw in the wheels, smokestack, smoke, and cowcatcher. Glue a button on for the rear wheel, and add the guest's name. Finished place card is shown in photo above, with pattern given below.

Button

Games

Crafty Fabric Game

Regardless of your sewing talent, you'll have no trouble with this game!

By Marcel Nechanicky, Buckingham, Iowa

SAVE scraps of each of the following types of fabric and give each guest a piece. Or, mount them on a board, and paste the following descriptions randomly on some type of board. Have each guest guess the answer that corresponds with the type of fabric mounted. See how many of your guests can guess!

tall story (yarn)
what fisherman use (net)
as good as cash (check)
bones heal this way (knit)
a musical instrument plus a girl's name (organdy)
two letters of the alphabet (pique—PK)
a fast dance plus a spot (polka dot)
part of the American flag (stripes)
a boy or girl's name (terry)
what wheat farmers do (grosgrain)
what fashionable ladies used to do (lace)
a letter of the alphabet plus a small boy (p-lad— plaid)
I give you permission (eyelet)
how a newspaper is used (red)

Laundry Day Relay

By Mary Jane Lamphier, Arlington, Iowa

DIVIDE THE group into two teams, and ask them to stand in a line at each end of a long table. Have a clothesline strung up somewhere in the room, either close to the table, or a few steps away. Put a diapered doll or teddy bear at each end of the table.

On the word "go", the first player in each line removes the diaper from the doll or bear, and hangs it on the clothesline with clothespins. The second player removes the diaper, and diapers the doll. The third removes the diaper from the doll, and places it on the clothesline, repeating this pattern until everyone on each team has played.

Plant Door Prizes

By Cathy Gondek, San Antonio, Texas

GREAT DOOR prizes for a tight budget are cuttings and tiny plants you've started yourself. Pick out the especially unusual ones!

Bib Relay

By Lynnette Stieben, Ness City, Kansas

DIVIDE THE guests into five groups, and give a baby bib to one person in each group. On the word "go" each group should start putting the bib on the next person in line, without help from the person being "bibbed". The first team to be "bibbed" from start to finish, wins.

Baby's Things

By Beth Tobler, Appleton, Wisconsin

UNSCRAMBLE these words. All are items connected with a baby and baby care. The person with the most correct answers wins.

1. ridepa (diaper)
2. gbgyu abyb (baby buggy)
3. tnifan ates (infant seat)
4. nobnte (bonnet)
5. rrmmtteeeoh (thermometer)
6. aknbetl (blanket)
7. rckreo (rocker)
8. obmlie (mobile)
9. dydte reba (teddy bear)
10. gnwogihtn (nightgown)
11. tartel (rattle)
12. cpaiifer (pacifier)
13. aceldr (cradle)
14. lesrtlor (stroller)
15. wdpore (powder)

Pins in the Oatmeal!

By Mrs. Loren Trunk, Princeton, Minnesota

THIS IS one of those fun shower games that is more difficult (and funny) than you'd imagine.

Mix 50 tiny gold safety pins in 1½ cups of rolled oats and place in a bowl. Blindfold each guest one at a time and give them 1 minute to see how many pins they can pick out of the oatmeal. The one who retrieves the most wins.

Busy Mother Game

More fun than you could imagine!

By Eva Segar, Hamilton, Missouri

HAVE TWO toy telephones, baby bottles, wash-cloths, and other items on hand for the contestants to "cope with".

Have the mother-to-be and the oldest mother, or the mother of the most children, change the diapers on the dolls.

As the hostess reads make-believe interruptions, the two contestants must successfully cope with them and get her doll diapered first, starting over again with each interruption.

For example: The hostess announces that the telephone is ringing. Each contestant must cradle the phone between her neck and ear while busily diapering the bouncing baby.

Others could be: The door bell rings and has to be answered, the baby's milk will be warm in one minute, the dog wants out, or the mother's toddler has to go potty.

Name Game

By Dorothy Peterson, Cashton, Wisconsin

HAVE YOUR guests fill in the blanks with names the new parents could give their baby—using the clue as a guide.

Boys' Names
1. not bald (Harry)
2. kind of cat (Tom)
3. not hot, not cold (Luke)
4. hair style (Butch)
5. what we receive each month to pay (Bill)
6. what we say to a gas attendant (Phil)
7. a movie mouse (Mickey)
8. a position of prayer (Neil)
9. far away (Miles)
10. kind of fabric (Terry)
11. the winner (Victor)
12. Eve's mate (Adam)
13. outspoken (Frank)
14. an automotive tool (Jack)

Girls' Names
1. a good way to cross a river (Bridget)
2. a precious stone (Ruby)
3. a book of the Bible (Esther)
4. another book of the Bible (Ruth)
5. happy and gay (Joy)
6. a kind of nut (Hazel)
7. a bird (Robin)
8. time of day (Eve)
9. a lady donkey (Jenny)
10. jewel of the sea (Pearl)
11. a month in summer (June)

12. flower - (violet)
13 flower - (rose)

Baby Jigsaw Puzzle

By Mildred Grenier, St. Joseph, Missouri

BEFORE THE shower, find several pictures of babies in magazines, cut them out and paste on cardboard. When dry, cut in jigsaw puzzle size pieces, with interesting shapes. Make several "puzzles", depending on how many guests you expect to attend. There should probably be several.

Scramble all the various puzzles' pieces together, and give each guest the same number of puzzle pieces when the time arrives for the game. Be sure to have card tables or some other working surface available. Guests must trade pieces until they have their baby correctly put together. The person or team that finishes first, wins.

Price the Item

By Bonnie Gazdag, Kalamazoo, Michigan

ARE YOU a smart shopper? How about your guests? This game will find out. Buy 5-10 items under $1 each. Have each guest write down what she thinks each costs. Afterwards, hold up each item again and give the group the actual price. The guests should write each down, and subtract the difference between her guess on that item and the actual price.

Have each total her "differences" and the one with the lowest figure wins. But give the items to the guest of honor!

What is a Baby Made of?

Snips, snails and puppy dog tails...

By Mrs. Randa Nill, Kulm, North Dakota

FILL in the blanks with words that match these descriptions.
1. The covering on an apple (skin)
2. Something grown on a stalk of corn (ear)
3. Something used by carpenters (nail)
4. Part of a bed (foot) or (head)
5. Narrow strip of land (neck)
6. Weapons of war (arms)
7. Branches of a tree (limbs)
8. Part of a clock (hands) or (face)
9. Part of a stovepipe (elbows)
10. Part of a wagon (tongue)
11. Sailor's consent (eye)
12. Major part of a comb (teeth)
13. To pull with a rope (toe)
14. Something to keep tools in (chest)
15. A type of macaroni (elbow)
16. A school child (pupil)
17. Tropical trees (palms)
18. What dogs bury (bones)
19. Place of worship (temple)
20. What the Tortoise raced with (hair)
21. Part of a river (mouth)
22. Name of an orange (navel)
23. An inquisitive person (nose)
24. To whip (lashes)
25. Spring flowers (two lips)
26. Part of a loaf of bread (heel)
27. Kind of bank account (joint)
28. To not use to good advantage (waist)
29. Kind of watch (wrist)
30. Part of celery (heart)

"Baby Things" Game

By Beth Tobler, Appleton, Wisconsin

USE AS many items as you like, giving more time for more items. If you'd like, give the items to the guest of honor after the game.

Gather together at least 20 or 25 baby items (Q-tips, rattles, Vaseline, powder, baby shampoo, diaper pins). Place the items in the middle of the floor, or pass on a tray, for all to see. Allow everyone to look at them for a few minutes. Remove the items from sight. Ask your guests to list as many of the items as they can.

Baby-O!

BEFORE the shower, make up as many player cards as you expect you'll need—either on large sheets of paper or 5 x 7-inch index cards. Write B-A-B-Y-O! across the top, and draw in spaces below the letters. Fill in the spaces differently on each card, using any number of the following words: Pins, diaper, thermometer, carry bed, training seat, bottle warmer, rubber pants, dress, baby bed, bassinet, buggy, crib, toy chest, etc.

Be sure to put a "free" space in the middle. After you make out the cards, make a master list of the words you used. Cut them apart and put in a container you can shake. Then pick out one word at a time, calling them aloud just as in Bingo. Use poker chips, buttons or pieces of paper for the players to place on their cards.

Entries too numerous to mention

Nursery Rhyme Quiz

By Mildred Grenier, St. Joseph, Missouri

REMEMBER the little rhymes your mother read you when you were a tot? Let's see how well they come back to you now. Fill in the rhyme or rhyme character appropriate for each of the following:
1. What little girl was quite obstinate? (Mary, Mary quite contrary)
2. Who ate with his fingers? (Little Jack Horner)
3. Who broke his crown? (Jack of Jack and Jill)
4. When was beef the highest it's ever been? (When the cow jumped over the moon)
5. Who was not a very good shepherdess? (Little Bo Peep, who lost her sheep)
6. Who should have been at home taking care of her children? (Ladybird)
7. Who had to jump high or he would have gotten burned? (Jack Be Nimble)
8. Who was frightened of insects? (Little Miss Muffett)
9. What man had trouble keeping his wife at home? (Peter, Peter Pumpkin Eater)
10. What couple didn't waste a bit of food? (Jack Sprat and his wife)
11. Who lived in an article of clothing? (The old woman who lived in a shoe)
12. Who went to sleep on the job? (Little Boy Blue)
13. What king liked to have music while he ate? (Old King Cole)
14. Whose father was a musician? (Tom, Tom the piper's son)

Baby Sing-along

This is great for shower laughs.

By Cathy Gondek, San Antonio, Texas

"Change Her Pants" (To the tune of "Row, Row, Row Your Boat")

Change, change, change her pants,
Twenty times a day,
Merrily, merrily, merrily, merrily,
Babies are that way.

Another, to the tune of "Twinkle, Twinkle Little Star"

(Put the new parents' name in, and put the appropriate number of children and a rhyming word, as well.)

Twinkle, twinkle, little star, how I wonder what you are.
Soon the *Rossings* will be *four,* with a baby to *adore.* (Or *three,* with their very own *baby*).
Twinkle, twinkle, little *girl;* babies can be such a *pearl* (or *tot;* babies sure are loved a *lot)*
Sometimes crying, sometimes wet, always lov-a-ble you bet,
Martha's lucky as can be, soon to have a new baby.

Surprise Diaper Door Prize

By Mrs. William Schmidt, Randolph, Wisconsin

WHEN YOU serve your refreshments, pass around a basket or tray of tiny folded diapers. Inside one, place a dab of peanut butter or mustard, making sure the "mess" is hidden from view. Later on, the one who gets the dirty diaper wins the door prize. But don't tell them until all the diapers are passed out!

Egg Surprise

By Mary Wood, Elvaston, Illinois

FILL a L'Eggs (panti-hose) container with several baby items and send it around the room. Have your guests guess what's inside and write them down. You'd be surprised how many things will fit! Cotton ball, teething disc, small toy, cotton swab, pacifier, aspirin, baby tooth, diaper pin, comb, barrette, sock, bootie, baby ring, rubber pants, etc. are just a few ideas.

Perhaps the funniest song is an admonition to the mother to sleep now because soon she won't have a chance! To the tune of "Rockabye Baby"

Rock-a-bye *Martha,* sleep while you may,
Soon you'll be busy both night and day.
Rachel's new *sister* (or *Martha's* new baby) soon will be here,
So rock-a-bye *Martha,* sleep for next year!

The favorite, however, will be your version of this next song, sung to the tune of "I've Been Working on the Railroad"

Mart's been working on a baby, all the live long day.
See her family growing larger, soon we'll hear our *Martha* say,
"Can't you learn to sleep the night through?"
Rise up so early in the morn.
Can't you hear the baby crying,
After she is born?
Baby, won't you sleep, baby, won't you sleep,
Baby, won't you sleep the whole night through?
Baby won't you sleep, baby won't you sleep,
Baby, won't you sleep all night?"
Martha's in the nursery with baby,
Martha's in the nursery, I know,
Martha's in the nursery with baby,
Strummin' on the ol' banjo,
And singin'...
La-la-la-lull-a-bye
La-la-la-lull-a-bye
La-la-la-lull-a-bye
Strummin' on the ol' banjo.

Farm Door Prizes

By Pat McCullough, Sharon, Wisconsin

WRAP YOUR farm gift attractively in saran wrap—everybody will wish she won!
  Some suggestions:
  dairy farm—a pound of butter
  egg farm—one dozen eggs
  cattle farm—one pound of hamburger
  produce farm—six large tomatoes
  hog farm—one pound of bacon
  poultry farm—a beautiful fryer
Other nice gifts and prizes would be jars of honey, jam, or homemade candy or cookies.

Telephone Quiz

Dial 3-8-6 for fun in this game.

By Judy Gerth, Princeton, Minnesota

PASS OUT copies of this telephone dial diagram and the list of numbers below. (Be sure to check your typing to make sure you have the correct numbers!) Set a time limit and have all the guests try to write in the word indicated by using the telephone dial.

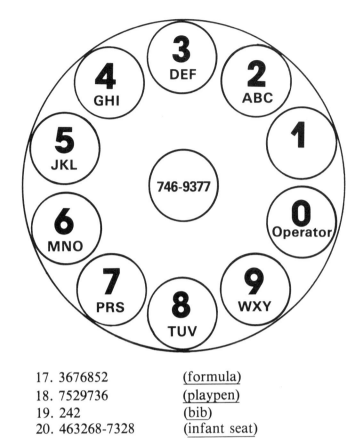

1. 342737   (diaper)
2. 268853   (bottle)
3. 4444-24247   (high chair)
4. 2668437   (booties)
5. 7533737   (sleeper)
6. 728853   (rattle)
7. 2868464   (bunting)
8. 7527842-72687 (plastic pants)
9. 2742   (crib)
10. 2229-645   (baby oil)
11. 2284463883   (bathinette)
12. 272353   (cradle)
13. 769337   (powder)
14. 2526538   (blanket)
15. 342737-7245   (diaper pail)
16. 266638   (bonnet)
17. 3676852   (formula)
18. 7529736   (playpen)
19. 242   (bib)
20. 463268-7328   (infant seat)

More Nursery Rhymes

By Cathy Gondek, San Antonio, Texas

HAVE YOUR guests complete the nursery rhymes after you read them aloud. The answers should be written.

1. Pat-a-cake, pat-a-cake, baker's man,
   Make me a cake as fast as you can:
   Pat it and prick it and mark it with B,
   And put it in the oven for baby and me.
2. Ride a cockhorse to Banbury Cross
   To see an old woman ride on a white horse.
3. I love little pussy, her coat is so warm
   And if I don't hurt her, she'll do me no harm.
4. Peas pudding hot, peas pudding cold,
   Peas pudding in the pot, nine days old.
   Some like it hot, some like it cold,
   Some like in in the pot, nine days old.
5. Hey! diddle diddle, the cat and the fiddle,
   the cow jumped over the moon,
   The little dog laughed to see such sport,
   While the dish ran after the spoon.
6. Little Tommy Tucker sang for his supper;
   What shall he eat? White bread and butter.
7. Little Jack Horner sat in a corner
   Eating a Christmas pie.
8. Old Mother Hubbard went to the cupboard,
   to get her poor dog a bone;
   But when she came there, the cupboard was
   bare, and so the poor dog had none.
9. Humpty Dumpty, sat on a wall;
   Humpty Dumpty had a great fall
   Not all the king's horses nor all the king's men
   could set Humpty Dumpty up again.
10. Simple Simon met a pieman, going to the fair
    Says Simple Simon to the pieman,
    "Let me taste your wares".
11. Baa, baa black sheep, have you any wool,
    Yes sir, yes sir, three bags full.
12. There was an old woman who lived in a shoe,
    She had so many children she didn't know
    what to do.

Car Pool Mom

Read these verses to shower guests.

By Barbara Stock, Wilmette, Illinois

Not rain nor sleet nor April balm
Shall halt the dauntless car pool Mom.
Through mumps and bumps she stays alive,
And counts the years 'til he can drive.

Growing Pains

By Barbara Stock, Wilmette, Illinois

My youngest son who's almost three
Prefers that I just let him be.
To skip his nap he thinks is best
But I'm the one who needs the rest.

New Baby

By Mrs. Glenn O. Tedrow, Fairfield, Iowa

Smaller than a tulip,
Softer than a rose,
But by love's secret miracle,
He has your eyes, my nose.
Is it not a marvel
How, with little fuss,
God has kept since Genesis
An exact blueprint of us?

What Will Stork Bring?

By Dorothy Peterson, Cashton, Wisconsin

HAND out blank paper, or draw a stork on several sheets of paper and leave blanks for the guests to fill in. (See example at right.)

Seal the papers in an envelope until the baby is born. The person with the closest guesses will get a small gift from either the party hostess or the new parents, whichever you choose.

Put as many "prediction" blanks on your stork as you'd like, starting with the phrase "The Stork will visit the Smith's home on (date), etc. Let your guests guess the baby's weight, hair and eye color, time of birth, sex and even future occupation and personality! Mom can read them in the hospital!

Which Baby Is Which?

By Beth Tobler, Appleton, Wisconsin

WHEN YOU send out invitations to your baby shower, ask each person to bring an unmarked photo of herself as a baby. As the guests arrive, tack or tape them to a bulletin board, and put a number under each one. Keep the board out of sight of the guests until time to play the game.

Hand out paper and pencils and ask each guest to write down which shower guest goes with which numbered photo, *without discussing aloud.*

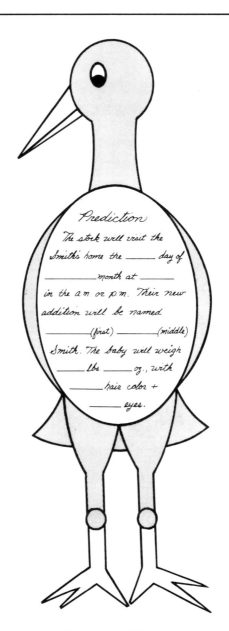

Prediction
The stork will visit the
Smith's home the _____ day of
_____ month at _____
in the a.m. or p.m. Their new
addition will be named
_____ (first) _____ (middle)
Smith. The baby will weigh
_____ lbs. _____ oz., with
_____ hair color +
_____ eyes.

It's a Girl! It's a Boy!

A real thinking game.

By Linda Stefoin, Albuquerque, New Mexico

THESE TWO puzzles may take a little while to complete, because there's only one clue given for each. But because you can check the right number of letters in each name listed against the spaces available, guests shouldn't have too much trouble.

It's a Girl Word List

3 letters
Ida
Sue

4 letters
Beth
Gail

5 letters
Anita
Carla
Diane
Ethel
Irene
Maria
Narda

6 letters
Agatha
Aileen
Carmel
Eunice
Ginger
Nicole
Norine
Phoebe
Theresa
Yvonne

7 letters
Abigail
Barbara
Bridget
Cecilia
Deborah
Heather
Pauline
Roxanne
Roberta
Vanessa

8 letters
Adrienne
Caroline
Lorraine
Madeline
Margaret
Nannette
Rosemary

9 letters
Alexandria
Annabelle
Geraldine
Katherine
Stephanie

It's a Boy Word List

3 letters
Ned

4 letters
Adam
Carl
Eric
Hugh
Matt
Paul
Pete
Zach

5 letters
Allen
Asher
Brett
Damon
Jason
Jerry
Lance
Rollo

6 letters
Adolph
Albert
Andrew
Arnold
Donald
Dwayne
Harold
Norman
Oliver
Palmer
Thomas
Vernon

7 letters
Abraham
Charles
Clement
Dominic
Isidore
Patrick
Raymond
Stewart
Timothy
Wallace
Zebulon

8 letters
Benjamin
Franklin
Hamilton
Jonathan
Lawrence
Nicholas
Octavius
Randolph

9 letters
Alexander
Maximilian
Nathaniel

11 letters
Christopher

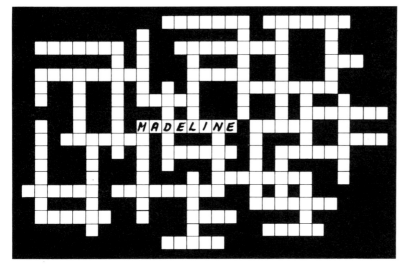

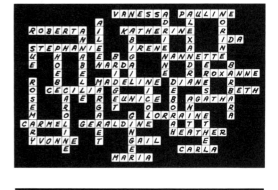

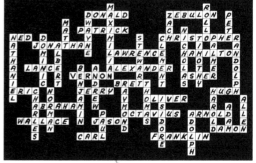

Nursery Crossword Puzzle

Fun and easy, this puzzle will be a light brainteaser for your guests.

By Cathy Gondek, San Antonio, Texas

Duplicate this puzzle and give a copy to each guest. Allow 5-10 minutes for the puzzle.

ACROSS

2 Used to walk a bigger baby
5 Used to clean small places like ears
7 Playthings
9 Rocking baby bed
10 Baby bed
13 Stuffed animal often called teddy
14 Newest member of the family
15 Fancy name for baby's wardrobe
17 Makes noise when baby shakes it
19 Sprinkled on baby's fanny
20 Periodic flip-flops of baby's tummy
23 Baby's first drink
24 Keeps baby dry
25 Device to help baby walk
27 Told to baby at bedtime
28 Occurs at 2 a.m. and other times

32 Device to capture precious moments forever
33 Night_____—helps you see in the dark
34 Rigid plan neither baby nor mother can follow
35 Bucket for soiled #24's across

DOWN

1 Without this, bottle is useless
2 Soft footwear inside shoes
3 Song sung to baby
4 Used to sit in while putting baby to sleep
6 Same as 2 across
8 Used to feed cereal
11 Used to walk baby outside
12 Place baby can play
14 Soft infant shoes
16 Baby's main communication
18 Until baby does this you must guess what she wants
21 Used when baby outgrows the bottle
22 Good place to rock baby outside
26 Used to hold milk
28 Bottle baby's drink
29 Girls' toy
30 Used to secure diapers
31 Round toy

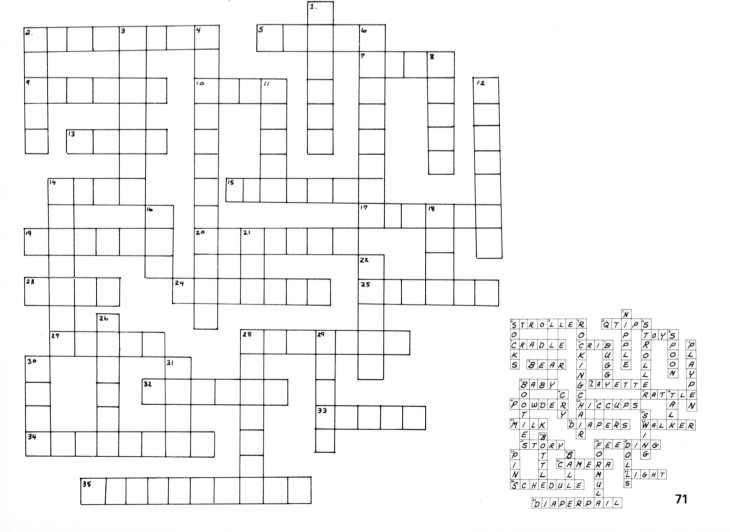

General Intelligence Test

Have your guests play this game while you get refreshments ready. The answers to the questions spell *"Refreshments Are Ready."*

By Judy Gerth, Princeton, Minnesota

FILL IN the spaces below with the answers to these questions:

1. If you ever saw the cow jump over the moon, write "no" in spaces 1, 4, 14 and 16. If not, write "R" in these spaces.

2. If "X" comes before "H" in the alphabet, write "Z" in space 3. If not write "F".

3. If 31,467 is more than 12 dozen write "E" in spaces 2, 5, 9, 15 and 17.

4. If you like candy better than mosquitoes, indicate with an "S" in spaces 6 and 12. If not, better consult an analyst.

5. Close one eye and without counting on your fingers write the eighth letter of the alphabet in space 7.

6. If Shakespeare wrote "Twinkle, twinkle little star, how I wonder what you are," write an "O" in space 20; otherwise, put a "Y" in that space.

7. If white and black are opposite write "M" in space 8. If they are the same color, write nothing there.

8. If ten quarts make one pint, draw an elephant in space 10. Otherwise write "N".

9. If summer is warmer than winter, put a "D" in space 19 and a "T" in space 11.

10. If you think this is foolish write the first letter of the alphabet in spaces 13 and 18 and then read the result.

1. _____	13. _____
2. _____	14. _____
3. _____	15. _____
4. _____	16. _____
5. _____	17. _____
6. _____	18. _____
7. _____	19. _____
8. _____	20. _____
9. _____	
10. _____	
11. _____	
12. _____	

Baby's Misspellings

By Mrs. Clifford Johnson, Owatonna, Minnesota

IN THE excitement of preparing this shower, a few important words were misspelled on this sheet of paper. Please help unscramble them so we'll all know what the new baby needs.

1. latter — (rattle)
2. sckolb — (blocks)
3. rapide — (diaper)
4. tablenk — (blanket)
5. nisatesbs — (bassinet)
6. dralec — (cradle)
7. ibcr — (crib)
8. ghih icrha — (high chair)
9. relace — (cereal)
10. kilm — (milk)
11. lumarof — (formula)
12. oeboti — (bootie)
13. gubgy — (buggy)
14. tlolrers — (stroller)
15. tubinng — (bunting)
16. promers — (rompers)
17. yappnel — (playpen)
18. tenbon — (bonnet)
19. baullly — (lullaby)
20. vole — (love)

Fruit and Vegetable Baby

By Dorothy Peterson, Cashton, Wisconsin

FOR THIS game, have your guests fill in the blanks with the names of fruits and vegetables. Only a short time is necessary.

When the baby arrives it will be as red as a (beet) but you won't (carrot) all. He/she may have (corn silk) hair, and a (turnip) nose, but he/she will be the (apple) of your eye. You will (squash) him/her to your breast and declare him/her a (peach). His dad will likely say (lettuce) make him/her king/queen for a day. Surely you will be a happy (pear).

How Big Is Momma?

By Eva Segar, Hamilton, Missouri

HAVE EACH guest guess the current measurements of the mother-to-be, writing her guess on a slip of paper. The one who comes closest to guessing the mother's waist measurements wins, but must give her prize to the expectant mother. A good prize would be something to make the mother feel pretty after she gets back her figure, like a nice belt or slimming skirt.

Blank Fever

Here's a fun thinking game that will give all your shower guests a good laugh!

By Ann Brower, Keota, Iowa

BLANK FEVER isn't a hard game to play, and it covers a variety of subjects so that if one person is poor in one category, she'll shine in another.

Each guest may play alone, or work with someone as a team. Provide paper and pencils for your guests. Prepare the sheets ahead of time, or let the shower guests do their own. For this, turn a sheet of paper horizontally, and write the word "CRADLE" across the top, leaving space between each letter.

In the margin on the left, write these categories: What Baby Wears, What Baby Plays With, Foods Baby Eats, Childhood Fictional Characters,

C R A D L E

	C	R	A	D	L	E
What Baby Wears	Cap	Rompers	Anklets	Diaper	Leggings	Embroidery
What Baby Plays with	Crayons	Rattle	Alphabet Blocks	Dolly	Lamb	(or) Elephant
Food Baby Eats	Cereal	Rice Pudding	Applesauce	Dog Biscuits	Lima Beans	Eggs
Childhood Fictional Characters	Cinderella	Rudolph the Reindeer	Aesop's Fables	Donald Duck	Lassie	Elves
What is in Baby's Room	Crib	Rubber Pants	Atomizer	Diaper Pail	Lamp	Enema Solution
Favorite Name (boy or girl)	Carla	Rosemary	Amy	Debbie	Linda	Edward

What's in Baby's Room, Favorite Name, etc.

The object of the game is for the guests to fill in the blank spaces with an appropriate answer for that category. The answer must begin with the letter at the top of the column.

Maternity Mix-Ups

By Laurie Norris, Hesperia, Michigan

UNSCRAMBLE THESE words to find out what the new "little one" will need in the nursery.

The Layette:
reapid	(diaper)
erppwra	(wrapper)
oetnnb	(bonnet)
teknalb	(blanket)
htsri	(shirt)
nnitgbu	(bunting)
oteboi	(bootie)

Baby's Food:
relace	(cereal)
kmli	(milk)
aertw	(water)
tifru	(fruit)
blatsevege	(vegetables)
tsato	(toast)
cijue	(juice)

Baby Furniture:
ttsseeniba	(bassinette)
icbr	(crib)
elacs	(scale)
htba	(bath)
ghih ricah	(high chair)
rrllotse	(stroller)
ylpaepn	(playpen)

Baby's Bath:
paso	(soap)
eordwp	(powder)
oottnc	(cotton)
zeaug	(gauze)
ilo	(oil)
weolt	(towel)
twrea	(water)

Animal Baby Names

By Mrs. Glenn Tedrow, Fairfield, Iowa

WRITE IN the "baby names" of each of these animals. The first person done with correct answers, wins.

bear (cub)	hog (piglet)
sheep (lamb)	deer (fawn)
duck (duckling)	elephant (calf)
frog (tadpole)	cat (kitten)
swan (cygnet)	seal (calf)
chicken (chick)	goose (gosling)
hen (pullet)	cow (calf)
stallion (colt)	cod (codling)
mare (filly)	

Gift Ideas

Alphabet Blocks

A beautiful, colorful gift mother and child will cherish for years.

(See photo on opposite page.)

By Mrs. Omar Stoutner, Keota, Iowa

Materials:
plastic "fashionese" needlepoint canvas
   (each block requires 6 3-inch squares)
yarn in various colors
jingle bells (optional)

CUT 3-inch squares of plastic needlepoint canvas. Embroider letters, such as B-A-B-Y on four of them. Now use your imagination for the remaining sides. Any charted design, such as a cross-stitch or needlepoint can be worked out on the mesh. When each square is done, put them together with an over and under weaving stitch along the edges.

If desired, put a jingle bell in one or more of the blocks for baby to enjoy.

These blocks would also make a clever centerpiece at the shower, and later could be given to the mother-to-be.

Bright-as-a-Button Baby Quilt

By Lisa Haas, Pipestone, Minnesota

Materials:
16 9-1/2 x 12-inch fabric blocks, in four
   different solid colors
contrasting fabric scraps
permanent felt pen
lightweight batting
quilt backing fabric
iron-on interfacing

CUT THE BLOCKS. (This size allows for a 1/2-inch seam.) The finished quilt will be four blocks wide and four blocks long.

Cut out the letters "B-A-B-Y", using the pattern (see page 98). Arrange the quilt blocks as you'd like them to appear, and place the letters for "Baby" diagonally from upper left to lower right. Alternate flowers and animals on the rest of the blocks, using the patterns (see page 98). Attach the letters and other figures with iron-on interfacing, and then use a machine zigzag stitch to permanently fasten them.

Use a permanent felt pen to color in the facial and floral features. Iron them on with a cloth soaked in water and vinegar to be sure they are permanent. Use a lightweight polyester batting as a fill, and back the quilt with gingham. Tie.

Wrapping Extra

By Mrs. Elroy Jensen, Canby, Minnesota

WRAP a large baby gift in a few yards of nursery-design cotton flannel. The new mother can make something for the baby to wear with it.

Don't Forget Dad!

By Mary Wood, Elvaston, Illinois

AT THE bottom of your shower invitations, add a note to ask each guest to bring a humorous gift for the new father (or the bridegroom!). He'll enjoy it.

Crazy Patch Bunny Quilt

Spread a little sunshine!

By Donna Rabe, Idaho Falls, Idaho

Materials:
tracing wheel
carbon paper
fabric scraps in assorted colors
background fabric (finished measurement
   will be 45 x 36 inches)
batting
trims
embroidery thread

TRACE THE bunny and bird parts onto fabric scraps, using a tracing wheel and carbon paper. (See pattern on page 100.) Experiment with different fabric textures to play out your quilt theme—using soft, furry-like fabric or anything that seems appropriate. Cut out. *Be sure to leave an allowance for turning under.*

Carefully press seam allowances under. Place on background fabric. Pin or baste securely and applique in place. After all pieces are sewn on, use a colorful embroidery thread to put a fancy edge on each piece of fabric. The quilt shown uses a buttonhole stitch.

Embroider daisies and grass on when finished. Back the quilt and trim with a lace edge if desired. Tie off.

After the baby is born, offer to embroider on the date, time, name and birth weight.

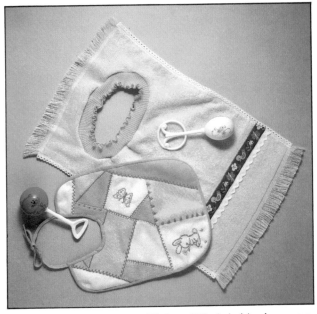

Directions for Pretty Thing Bib (pink) given on page 78.

Crazy Quilt Bib

By Jo Wenzel, Kent, Illinois

Materials:
knit scraps of similar weight and texture
embroidery floss
embroidery patterns (or make your own)
terry cloth
bias tape to match

MACHINE PIECE the knit scraps together. Randomly stitch rectangles, triangles, etc. to make a piece measuring 9 x 12 inches. Cut this piece into a bib shape. (See pattern on page 102.) Machine stitch around the edge to keep seams from pulling apart.

Use embroidery floss to topstitch each seam. (Check a stitchery book for possible stitches.) Add an embroidered figure in a section or two, if desired. Once the topstitching is completed, simply bind the terry and bib top with bias tape trim.

Hand stitch the trim down in back for a clean finish.

This will be a perfect dress up bib when baby is away visiting with grandparents!

Crawling Baby Quilt

Why not make a cute baby quilt with the baby crawling and exploring?

By Donna Rabe, Idaho Falls, Idaho

Materials:

tracing wheel	trims
carbon paper	batting
diaper fabric	embroidery thread
fabric scraps	5-1/2 x 4-1/2-inch cardboard

background fabric (finished measurement will be 45 x 36 inches)

TRACE the baby and blocks onto fabric scraps, using a tracing wheel and carbon paper and the pattern on page 100. Cut out.

Make the baby blocks, using a 5-1/2 x 4-1/2-inch cardboard pattern. Pin or baste the pieces in place, and applique onto the already-quilted backing. Embroider the baby blocks with brightly colored embroidery floss.

Use rickrack trims and ribbon to dress up the baby bonnet, and quilt border.

Use extra batting under the diaper, bonnet and blocks—this will make the quilt baby "come to life" in a three-dimensional way.

Embroider tiny toes and the clasp of the diaper pin. Back and finish the quilt, attaching a gathered edging.

Yo-Yo Mobile

By Mary Allen, Plymouth, New Hampshire

Materials:
fabric scraps
thread
yarn
rickrack
dowels or a coat hanger

CUT ANY size circle you want from several scraps of fabric—6 inches in diameter is a manageable size. Turn the edge under about 1/4 inch. Press. With double thread, stitch around the edge with large stitches. Gather the fabric tightly as you work.

When the yo-yo is fully gathered, make a few extra stitches to secure the thread. Make several colors and sizes if you wish.

Sew yarn or rickrack to the back of each and attach mobile-style to narrow wooden dowels or a coat hanger. Hang where it will catch the breeze and baby's eye.

Appliqued Towels for Baby

Any new mother would appreciate a cheery vest or set of towels.

By Jo Wenzel, Kent, Illinois

Materials:
a pastel-colored towel/washcloth set
a terry cloth diaper shirt
calico fabric scraps
solid fabric scraps
iron on polyweb fabric

USE THE patterns (see page 101) to make the figures shown. Iron onto the towel using the polyweb (or pin in place). Use a zigzag stitch to applique in place. Add trim to the cow's face with fabric paint or embroidery floss.

By using these farmyard prints on your towel set, you'll be giving a gift of your talents and of your lifestyle (if you're a farm family!)

Coming Home Gift

By Betty Siemers, Grand Island, Nebraska

WRAP your baby shower gift in a receiving blanket, and instead of ribbon and tape, use diaper pins, and a rattle tied with a bow.

"Pretty Thing" Bib

By Mrs. Thomas Nelsen, Jr., Estherville, Iowa

(See photo on page 76)

Materials:
pastel-colored hand towel
1-1/2 feet of stretch knit trim (as shown on bib on page 76) to match
various fabric trims, rickrack, etc.

CUT a 6-1/2-inch wide oval neck opening about 2-1/2 inches from one end of the towel, measuring from the fringe.

Baste on a pretty stretch knit trim. This will ruffle nicely. Trim the long edges of the towel bib with a pretty white trim, and stitch wide rickrack and a fanciful "childrens'" trim across the bottom edge, about 4 inches from the fringe at the other end of the towel.

The mother-to-be will love the bib and she'll always think of you when it is used. And it's so easy to put on and take off.

Elephant Crib Toy

By Carla Read, Henry, Illinois

Materials:
felt scraps
1 yard of grosgrain ribbon for each elephant
fiberfill

USING pattern (see page 102) cut out two elephant body pieces and four ear pieces for each elephant. With right sides together, stitch ears, clip curves, trim and press.

Attach ears to elephant body at line shown on pattern, leaving the ear toward the elephant trunk. Tack in place. Press toward back.

With right sides together, stitch elephant. Leave an opening between the x's. Clip curves, trim and turn. Stuff with fiberfill or some other lightweight filling. Slip stitch opening. Stitch on button for eye. Attach ribbon to elephant and tie to side of crib. Or, make several for a mobile!

Baby Animal Mobile

Charm the newborn infant with this cheerful, pom-pom mobile.

By Heather Lambrecht, Maple Valley California

(See knot illustrations on page 81.)

Materials:
45 yards of 6-ply acrylic yarn or maxi-cord (Cut 8 5-yard cords; 1 2-yard cord and 1 3-yard cord.)
1 1-1/2-inch metal ring
1 9-inch metal ring
4 baby blocks with holes drilled through their centers
5 pom-pom animals (the pom-pom animals can be purchased ready-made at craft and hobby stores or you can buy ready-made pom-poms and put the animals together yourself.)

Mobile

Pull the eight 5-yard cords through a 1-1/2-inch ring at their midpoints. Use the 2-yard cord to wrap these cords together for 2 inches directly under the ring.

Tie eight chinese crown knots.

Divide your cords into four groups with four cords in each group. Number the cords from 1-16. On cords 1-4 and 9-12 tie 4 inches of square knots (see illustration) using two filler cords and two corking cords in each group.

On cords 5-8 and 13-16 tie 4 inches of half knots, also using two filler cords and two working cords in each group.

Add a baby block to each sinnet pushing all four cords through the hole in the baby block.

On cords 1-4 and 9-12 tie 5-1/2 inches of square knots. On cords 5-8 and 13-16 tie 5-1/2 inches of half knots.

Double half-hitch cords 1-16 onto the 9-inch ring. Finish wrapping the ring with the 3-yard cord.

Tie two square knots on each group of four cords below ring using two filler cords and two working cords in each group. Trim cord to 4 inches below ring. Unravel cord and brush to fluff.

Hang a pom-pom animal between each group of cords. Attach the biggest animal to the center of the crown knots inside the ring. Needle and thread work well to hang the animals with. If the animals don't balance properly, glue a piece of floral wire along the center of their bottoms.

(Patterns for other animals on next page.)

Pom-Pom Blue Dolphin

Materials:
4 2-inch light blue pom-poms
2 1-1/2-inch light blue pom-poms
1 1-inch light blue pom-pom
2 10-millimeter "roller-baller" eyes
dark blue felt for fins and tail
clear-drying craft glue

Glue the pom-poms together as shown in the arrangement below.

Cut top fin, tail and two side fins out of blue felt using patterns on page 102.

Glue tail under 1-inch pom-poms. Glue top fin between two center 2-inch pom-poms. Glue side fins on either side of front 2-inch pom-pom. Glue eyes on either side of front 1-1/2-inch pom-pom.

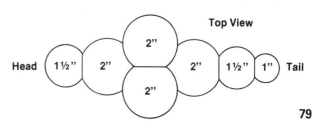

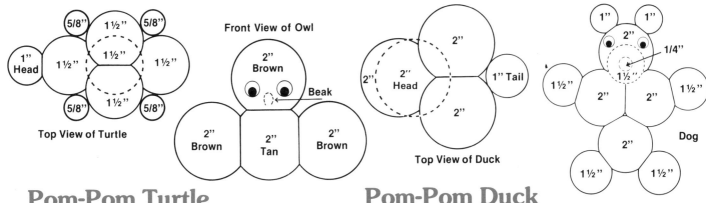

Pom-Pom Turtle

Materials:
5 1-1/2-inch dark green pom-poms
1 1-inch light green pom-pom
4 5/8-inch light green pom-poms
green felt for tail
2 10-millimeter "roller-baller" eyes
clear-drying craft glue

Arrange 1-1/2-inch pom-poms as shown above.
Glue the fifth one on top in the center. Glue the rest of the pom-poms as shown. Glue tail at the back end.
Cut one of tail pattern shown on page 102.
Glue eyes on the 1-inch light green pom-pom.

Pom-Pom Owl

Materials:
3 2-inch brown pom-poms
1 2-inch tan pom-pom
2 10-millimeter "roller-baller" eyes (available in craft shops)
scrap of orange felt for beak
clear-drying craft glue

Glue pom-poms as shown above.
Glue eyes to lower part of top brown pom-pom.
Cut out beak using pattern on page 102.
Pinch beak in half and glue between eyes.

Pom-Pom Duck

Materials:
4 2-inch yellow pom-poms
1 1-inch yellow pom-pom
2 10-millimeter "roller-baller" eyes
orange felt for beak
clear-drying craft glue

Glue the three large and one small pom-poms as shown above.
Place the remaining large one on top of one of the end pom-poms, as shown. This is the duck's head. Glue the eyes on the top pom-pom.
Cut two bills using pattern on page 102.
Glue the bills in place, one over the other.

Pom-Pom Brown Dog

Materials:
4 2-inch brown pom-poms
5 1-1/2-inch brown pom-poms
2 1-inch brown pom-poms
1 1/4-inch brown pom-pom (for nose)
2 10-millimeter "roller-baller" eyes
ribbon for bow
clear-drying craft glue
felt scrap (pink) for tongue

Glue all the pom-poms as shown above.
Glue the eyes on the topmost 2-inch pom-pom.
Attach the ribbon around dog's neck.

Remember Dad?

By Evelyn Tuller, Elwood, Kansas

MOTHER and baby are going to be well-remembered at shower-time, but how about making a special package for the expectant father?

Fix a special little package to help him through those hospital hours, including a packet of dimes, a list of telephone numbers, a couple of candy bars and package of gum, a paperback book, a magazine or two and a deck of cards. He will appreciate your thoughtfulness.

Baby Soaps and Washcloths

By Anna Mary Yoder, Middlebury, Indiana

Materials:
terry cloth fabric · baby soaps
bias seam binding · old magazines

CUT fabric into 5-inch squares, and sew seam binding around the edges to make cloths.

Decoupage cute pictures (cut from magazines and wrapping paper) onto the soaps. Arrange soap and cloths in a small gift box.

Macrame Knot Illustrations

(Use these with Baby Animal Mobile on pages 79-80.)

Chinese Crown Knot

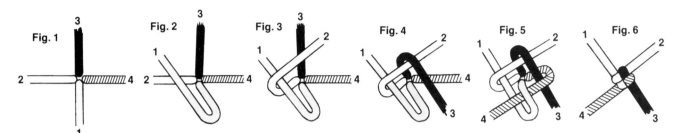

Figure 1: Hold all cords upside down in your fist. Divide the cords into four equal groups. Put one group behind your thumb. This is group 1. Number other groups clockwise 2, 3 and 4.

Figure 2: Pick up group 1 and lay over group 2. Drop group 1 as you pick up group 2.

Figure 3: Lay group 2 over group 3. Drop group 2 and pick up group 3.

Figure 4: Lay group 3 over group 4. Drop group 3 and pick up group 4.

Figure 5: Lay group 4 over group 3, then put it through the hole where your thumb is. Remove your thumb and tighten each group of cords separately.

Figure 6: This is how the finished knot should look.

Square Knot

Figure 1: Cords 1 and 4 are working cords. Cords 2 and 3 are filler cords.

Figure 2: Half Knot

Figure 1 and Figure 2 of the Square Knot make a half knot.

Figure 3: Square knot before working cords are pulled tight.

Figure 4: This is what the completed square knot looks like when the working cords are pulled tight.

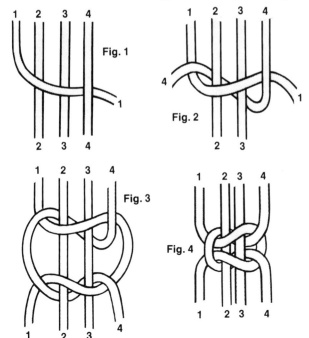

Double Half Hitch

Figure 1: Tie cords together as shown.

Figure 2: Pull the first or left loop tight.

Figure 3: Pull the right loop tight, and this is what the finished knot looks like.

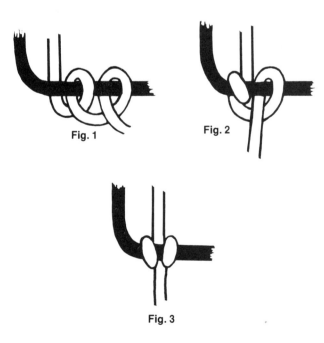

Baby Booties

A handmade pair of knitted booties is the perfect, sentimental gift.

By Mary Lamb Becker, Shorewood, Wisconsin

(See knitting abbreviations on page 2.)

Size: Infant to 6 months
Yarn: 1-1/2 ounces Sportweight
Needles: 1 pair single pointed needles in size you require to reach gauge of 6 stitches (sts) = 1 inch
Other materials: Blunt yarn needle, four stitch markers
(Note: Bootie is knit from bottom up. Number of stitches after an increase or decrease row are indicated in parentheses at end of that row.)

Cast on 38 sts divided by markers as follows: 3 sts, marker, 10 sts, marker, 12 sts, marker, 10 sts, marker, 3 sts.

Row 1: K 3, sl marker, inc in next st, k 8, inc in next st, sl marker, k 12, sl marker, inc in next st, k 8, inc in next st, sl marker, k 3 (42).
Row 2: P.
Row 3: K, inc after first and third markers and before second and fourth markers as in row 1 (46).
Row 4: P.
Row 5: K, inc 4 sts as in row 3 (50).
Row 6: P, removing all markers.
Row 7: K 18, inc in next st, k 12, inc in next st, k 18 (52).
Rows 8, 9 and 10: P.
Row 11: K 18, k 3 tog from front (i.e. insert right needle from left to right through third, second and first sts in that order and k tog), k 10 sl next st as if to k, return to left needle, giving st half twist to right, k 3 tog through back loops (i.e. insert right needle from right to left through back loops of first, second and third sts in that order and k tog), k 18 (48).
Row 12: P.
Row 13: K 16, k 3 tog from front (as in row 11), k 10, turn st and k 3 tog through back

loops (as in row 11), k 16 (44).
Row 14: P.
Row 15: K 14, k 3 tog from front (as in row 11), k 10, turn st and k 3 tog through back loops (as in row 11), k 14 (40).
Row 16: P.
Row 17: K 12, k 3 tog from front (as in row 11), k 10, turn st and k 3 tog through back loops (as in row 11), k 12 (36).
Row 18: P.
Row 19: K 10, k 3 tog from front (as in row 11), k 10, k 3 tog through back loops (as in row 11), k 10 (32).
Row 20: P.
Row 21: K 1, *k 2 tog, yo. Rep from * 13 times more. End with k 2 tog, k 1.
Row 22: P all sts and yo's (31).
Rows 23-34: K 1, p 1 across, ending with k 1. Bind off all sts and break yarn, allowing 27 inches for seaming. Fold bootie at center front and sew center back seam and sole seam.

Tie: Measure 6 yards of yarn, fold in half and use doubled. Make sl knot on crochet hook and ch for 16 ins. Break yarn and pull loop on hook until end slips through. Weave yarn ends into chain using blunt yarn needle. Thread chain through beading row of bootie at ankle and tie in bow. Rep for second bootie.

Diaper Wrap

By Mrs. Elroy Jensen, Canby, Minnesota

WRAP a smaller gift in a new fabric diaper and fasten with baby safety pins and a rattle.

Something Extra

By Mrs. Elroy Jensen, Canby, Minnesota

GIVE a diaper bag with a little something tucked inside—a box of baby cereal, toys, etc.

Sunsuit

Make a baby sunsuit for a personal, *useful* gift. It's easy, too.

By Carla Read, Henry, Illinois

ALL SEAMS are about 3/8 inch. You'll need about 1 yard of fabric. Pin pattern (see page 103) to the fabric on the straight grain, and cut. Stitch center front and center back seams. Finish with a serging stitch to keep seams from raveling.

Stitch shoulder straps. Turn and press. Topstitch. Baste to back of sunsuit at an angle. (Adjust so strap will smoothly reach the front.)

Stitch back facing to sunsuit back. Clip curves, turn and press.

Stitch front facing to sunsuit front. Clip curves, turn and press.

Stitch side seams. Press facing down around top of sunsuit. Topstitch entire top portion.

Stitch crotch area again to reinforce. Make casings at leg openings of about 3/8 inch. Run 1/8-inch elastic through the casing (measure to fit baby's leg, but should be about 7-7-1/2-inches). Secure elastic and close casing.

Use gripper snaps to attach straps to front.

Baby Romper

By Carla Read, Henry, Illinois

ALL SEAMS are about 3/8 inch wide. This pattern requires about 1/2-yard of stretch fabric. (See pattern page 104.) Romper fits baby from 9-15 pounds.

Pin pattern to fabric on straight grain, and cut. Stitch center front and center back seams. (Use wider seams for a smaller baby.) Stay stitch neck edge.

For center front band, cut a strip of fabric the same length as the center front seam, about 2-2-1/2 inches wide. Fold to desired width and press edges under. Baste to romper front, centering over front seam.

Baste each edge of band about 1/8 inch from the edge. Add a decorative stitch or edging. Press.

Stitch shoulder seams. Press.

Using bias tape or material cut on the bias (and folded like bias tape), bind neck and neck opening. Add a decorative stitch or edging, and closing.

Baste sleeve top to ease in. Stitch sleeves to romper. Add decorative touches.

Stitch side seam and underarm seam through the end of sleeve. Clip curves, trim and press. Hem sleeves.

Press 1/8 to 1/4 inch under on crotch. Fold another 1/2 inch under and press. Baste. Do this on both front and back crotch edges.

Make leg casings about 1/4 to 3/8 inches wide. Run 1/8-inch elastic through the casing and adjust to fit leg. (Should be about 7-1/2 inches.) Secure elastic at each end of casing.

Use gripper snaps to close crotch. (Use No. 16 snaps on either side of the center seam and No. 14 snaps near the legs.)

Baby's Memory Album

By Laurie Norris, Hesperia, Michigan

PLACE A note in each invitation asking the guest to bring a favorite baby poem and a clipping of a baby from a magazine with her to the baby shower.

As each guest arrives, give her one page from an album and have the guest design her own page, placing on it the picture and poem, and whatever other touches she may want to add.

Make sure each guest signs her name at the bottom of the page she creates. Some guests may want to write a special poem for the baby and mother-to-be. When all the guests have completed their pages, put them together in an album and give the book to the mother-to-be as a keepsake.

Felt Baby Book

This cute little pocketed fabric book will pull at your heartstrings. (Directions for other book opposite.)

By Carla Read, Henry, Illinois

Materials:
2 5 x 13-inch pieces of felt
12-inch piece of rickrack
felt scraps
2 5 x 12-1/2-inch pieces of felt
embroidery thread
permanent waterproof marking pen
several cotton balls

CUT TWO large pieces of felt to make the book cover. Each should measure about 5 x 13 inches. Pink the edges. On one piece, stitch the "baby pocket". Baste a pretty piece of rickrack to the point on the cover where the book folds. (This will attach to the baby.) With right sides together, stitch the front and back pieces together, leaving an opening to turn. Turn, press and slip stitch opening. (See patterns on pages 97, 98 and 99.)

Cut two pieces measuring 5 x 12-1/2 inches for inside pages. Mark the center of these with pins so you'll have 4 5 x 6-1/4-inch pages.

On one, stitch the buggy and on the opposite side, stitch the crib. *(Remember:* Stitch only three edges of each page decoration so the felt baby can sit inside each.) Add a rattle to the buggy, a teddy bear to the crib. (Use a narrow zigzag stitch.)

On the other "page", stitch the high chair, stitching the chair back, legs and rungs. Attach the tray, stitching only three sides. Add bottle.

On the opposite side of the page, stitch three sides of the tub. With a waterproof marker, draw on drops of water coming from the faucet and bubbles. Add felt duck.

If you wish, add captions on each page such as: "This book belongs to _____"; "Let's take a walk"; "Time to eat"; "Bath time"; "Time for Bed"; and "This book was handmade by (name) (date). Use waterproof markers for writing, or embroider. Draw on the features of the teddy bear, duck, bottle, rattle, etc.

To make the baby, use flesh-colored felt. Cut one circle in the flesh-colored felt, and one in a hair color. Draw on a face. With *wrong* sides together, stitch narrow zigzag stitch around the edge, leaving a tiny opening at the chin to stuff. Stuff with cotton balls.

Cut two pieces for the body, using any color desired. Stitch around the outside, using the narrow zigzag stitch, and leaving an opening at the neck. Stuff. Insert head into body and pin. Insert end of rickrack piece. Zigzag together.

Here are two little fabric books any baby would love to flip through.

Begin with a special word to baby, and an invitation to take a walk.

A high chair and bottle for baby's use, and two little ducks for play.

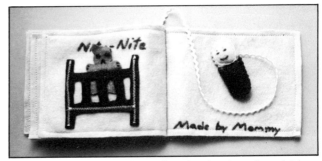
Time for bed in this cute little crib and a signature of special love.

Gingham Heart Pillow

Cute to look at and to hold!

By Donna Rabe, Idaho Falls, Idaho

Materials:

fabric scraps	embroidery thread
thick batting	lace or eyelet trim

SEW TOGETHER two (or several) colors of gingham blocks. When your piece is large enough, use a large Valentine candy box as a pattern and cut out a large heart from the gingham-square fabric just created.

From a larger piece of solid color gingham, cut a second heart-shaped piece. This is the back of pillow. From a square of bonded batting, cut another heart the same size. Pin the batting heart to the patchwork heart. Tie in the corners of each square.

After the pieces are tied together, baste the batting to the pillow top. Sew pre-ruffled lace or eyelet around the pillow. Now sew the backing onto the top, leaving about 5 inches open to stuff your pillow.

After pillow is stuffed, slip stitch opening shut.

Baby's First Fabric Book

By Jo Wenzel, Kent, Illinois

Materials:

several yards, or scraps, of solid-color polyester knit fabric
2 pieces of denim, each about 7 x 9 inches
various fabric trims (ribbon, rickrack, etc.)
fabric crayons
steam iron

BEFORE the shower, assemble a "book" with polyester knit pages (one for each guest) (see book at upper left on page 84). Stitch together, and bind in a durable, denim cover. Make neat edges. Add fabric trims and stitching to make the pages more colorful. (A good finished book size is about 7 x 9 inches.)

The hostess should make a list of things the baby would enjoy looking at (animals, a farm scene, etc.) and letter the pages (dog, cat, etc.) before the shower.

When the guests arrive, pass a hat with the page themes written on paper. Have the guests "draw" which page they'll make.

To make the pages: Use fabric crayons. Have your guests draw on paper (writing in reverse).

Turn the paper over and trace letters and drawings with the fabric crayon. (This is important because ironing the letters without transferring them from original sketch to fabric would make the letters and drawings backwards!)

The colors will be very vivid and bright when transferred onto the fabric—experiment before-hand to make sure iron is hot enough. (Or, iron the drawings on after the party and give the book to the mother-to-be later.)

(See page 84 for cover photo.)

Animal Baby Bib

A cute bit of imagination!

By Mrs. Don Schwartz, Winneton, Nebraska

Materials:
large washcloths (one for each bib)
polyester fabric scraps
thread
bias seam tape

TURN THE top two corners of a washcloth down and tack in place. Add eyes, mouth and nose from fabric scraps. Cut the bottom corners of the washcloth to have a rounded edge, and finish entire bib edge with a zigzag stitch. Add bias seam tape at top for bib ties.

When baby outgrows the bib, the ears can be untacked and the bib becomes a washcloth again!

Dress Up Baby Shirt

By Carla Read, Henry, Illinois

IF YOU don't have time to make an outfit for the new baby, why not decorate some purchased baby T-shirts for the new parents? It would be a thoughtful and practical gift.

Buy a package of T-shirts, and zigzag stitch on brightly-colored thread designs around the neck, sleeve edges and wherever you'd like. If you'd like to be even more creative, embroider the shirts to go with baby's "good" clothes.

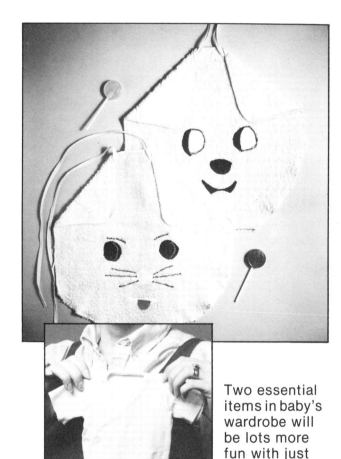

Two essential items in baby's wardrobe will be lots more fun with just a little dressing up. Trim your bibs and T-shirts as described at left.

Sock Corsage

By Mrs. Rodney Voelker, Brownsdale, Minnesota

Materials:
3 pairs baby socks in different colors
6 stems of artificial rose leaves
florist's tape

ROLL each sock from toe to the top of cuff. Roll the cuff down around the rolled-up sock to form the outside petal of the rose. If the socks you're using have print on them, be sure to turn them inside out so the print won't show.

Wrap florist's tape around the bottom of each "flower" and attach to a leaf stem with florist's tape. Wrap them all together. The mother can use the corsage later for her baby.

"Cutie Pie" Bootie

The bootie pictured at top on page 88 will delight your shower guests.

By Linda Trexler, Germansville, Pennsylvania

(See crochet abbreviations on page 2.)

Materials:

Plastic or cardboard container

1 ounce knitting worsted weight yarn (for bootie of approximately 6 x 5 x 4 inches)

1/2 ounce sport or "baby" weight yarn for trim

Paper punch

Size H crochet hook, or size needed to reach gauge of 4 double crochet per inch, using knitting worsted. Second hook one or two sizes smaller for trim.

Yarn needle

Fabric scraps

Glue

TO PREPARE carton, cut into bootie shape as indicated by Figure 1, saving scraps for instep. Mark every half inch along upper edge between points 1 and 2 and around toe between points 3 and 4. Punch hole at each mark.

Row 1: Beg at point 1 with outside of bootie towards you, work sc in first hole as follows: With sl knot on hook, insert hook into hole and draw loop back (Figure 2). Yarn over and draw through both loops on hook (Figure 3). This is one sc completed. Make 2 more sc in same hole. Make 2 sc in each of remaining holes along upper edge except last one. Make 3 sc in last hole.

Row 2: Ch 3, turn. Working in back loop only, dc in each st of previous row. Rep row 2 until piece reaches points 3 and 4, working in front and back loops on alternate rows to produce a ridge on right side.

Remainder of bootie is worked in rounds. Turn bootie right side up. Depending on size of container and, consequently, number of rows worked, your hook could be at either point 3 or point 4.

If at point 3, work from inside of bootie, 2 sc through each of the holes along toe. Slip st to first dc of previous row. Ch 3. With bootie upside down, work dc in back loop only through dc's of previous row and sc's along toe. Sl st to ch 3 at beg of rnd. Continue dc in back loop only, beg each rnd with ch 3 and closing rnd with sl st into ch 3, until crochet reaches "sole" of bootie.

If at point 4, work from outside of bootie, 2 sc in each of holes along toe. Sl st to first dc of previous row. Ch 3. With bootie upside down, work dc in front loop only through dc's of previous row and sc's along toe. Sl st to ch 3 at beg of rnd. Continue dc in front loop only, beg each rnd with ch 3 and closing rnd with sl st into ch 3 until crochet reaches "sole" of bootie.

Work one more row of sc, dec 6-10 sts. Break yarn and fasten. With threaded yarn needle, catch sts on opposite sides of sole, using long sts across sole to hold crochet to bottom of bootie.

INSTEP

From scraps of container, cut rectangle that will reach across instep of bootie, extending about 1/2-3/4 inch over sides. Allow for an "open toe" effect (see photo on next page).

Punch holes along two long sides of rectangle spaced as for bootie.

Row 1: Work 1 row of sc through holes along one of long sides, with 3 sc in first and last holes, 2 sc in all other holes.

Row 2: Ch 3, turn. Work dc in each st of previous row. Rep row 2 until entire instep piece is covered. Attach last completed row to remaining holes by sewing. Work shell st around all four sides of instep.

Shell stitch: Join contrasting yarn. With smaller hook, ch 3, work 5 dc in next st, skip st, *sc in next st, skip st, 6 dc in next st, skip st. Rep from *. Sl st to ch 3 at beg of rnd.

Trim rest of bootie as follows: Beg at point 4 and moving toward toe, work sl st for distance equal to shorter measurement of instep piece. Beg working shell st around tip of toe, changing back to sl st for same distance before reaching point 3. Continue working shell st up to point 1, around top of bootie to point 2, and down to point 4. Break yarn and fasten. (Glue scrap fabric to inside of bootie for lining.) Sew instep to bootie, allowing opening at toe.

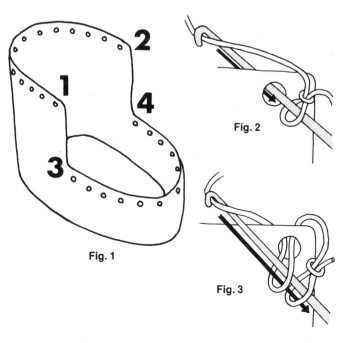

Fig. 1

Fig. 2

Fig. 3

Pretty Baby Bassinet

The crocheted bassinet (bottom of photo) is fun to make.

By Linda Trexler, Germansville, Pennsylvania

(See crochet abbreviations on page 2.)

Materials:

Plastic or cardboard container

1 ounce of knitting worsted weight yarn (for bassinet of approximately 6 x 4 x 4 inches)

1/2 ounce of sportweight or "baby" weight yarn for trim

Paper punch

Size H crochet hook, or size needed to reach gauge of 4 double crochet per inch using knitting worsted

Second hook one or two sizes smaller for trim

Yarn needle

Scrap fabric

Glue

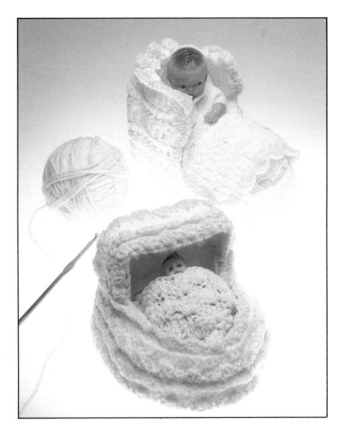

CUT BASSINET shape from container as indicated in figure below. Punch holes as indicated on drawing, spacing every half inch.

TOP

Row 1: Work 2 sc through each hole between points 1 and 2, with 3 sc in first and last holes. Work with outside of bassinet toward you.

Row 2: Ch 3, turn. Dc in each st of previous row working in back loop. Rep row 2 until rectangle formed by points 1, 5, 6 and 2 is covered. Alternate rows are worked in front and back loops creating a ridge on right side. Break yarn and fasten.

SIDES

Join yarn at point 2. With right side of work toward you, work dc along edge to point 6, continue on to point 5, ending at point 1. Ch 3, turn. Work dc back and forth through front or back loops in alternate rows until crochet reaches points 3 and 4.

SKIRT

Turn bassinet right side up. Depending on size of container and, consequently, number of rows worked, your hook could be at either point 3 or point 4.

If at point 3, work from inside of bassinet, 2 sc through each hole along upper edge of bassinet. Sl st to first dc of previous row. Ch 3. With bassinet upside down, work dc in back loop only through dc's of previous row and sc's along upper edge of bassinet skirt. Sl st to ch 3 at beg of rnd. Continue dc in back loop only, beg each rnd with ch 3 and closing rnd with sl st into ch 3, until crochet reaches bottom of bassinet.

If at point 4, work from outside of bassinet. Work 2 sc in each of holes along upper edge of bassinet skirt. Sl st to first dc of previous row. Ch 3. With bassinet upside down, work dc in front loop only through dc's of previous row and sc's along upper edge of bassinet. Sl st to ch 3 at beg of rnd. Continue dc in front loop only, beg each rnd with ch 3 and closing rnd with sl st into ch 3 until crochet reaches bottom of bassinet.

To finish bassinet, work 1 row of shell st along lower edge of skirt and around bonnet and upper edge of cradle.

Shell stitch: Join contrast yarn. With smaller hook, ch 3, work 5 dc in next st, skip st, *sc in next st, skip st, 6 dc in next st, skip st. Rep from *. Sl st to ch 3 at beg of rnd.

Additional rows of shell sts can be worked as desired. Glue scrap fabric to inside of cradle for lining. Add mattress, doll baby and quilt cover of any fancy crochet stitch.

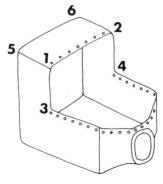

Whirly Bird Cap

This is a great baby shower gift you can make up in no time at all.

By Mary Lamb Becker, Shorewood, Wisconsin

(See knitting abbreviations on page 2.)

Size: 16-inch head size
Yarn: 2 ounces of 4-ply knitting worsted weight; 1/2 ounce knitting worsted weight in contrasting color.
Gauge: In stockinette stitch using larger needles, 5 stitches (sts) per inch.
Needles: 1 pair single point in size 8 or size needed to reach gauge; 1 pair single point two sizes smaller for ribbing; 1 blunt-pointed yarn needle; size J or K crochet hook.

RIBBED CUFF

With smaller size needles, cast on 80 sts. Work in ribbing of k 1, p 1 until piece measures 1-1/2 ins. Change to larger size needles.

CAP BODY

Work even in ss until piece measures 7 ins from cast on. End with p row.

EMBROIDERY TRIM

With work still on needle, thread yarn needle with contrasting color and embroider 7 vertical rows of chain stitch. These embroidered rows should be spaced every 10 sts. (Note: There are no chain sts embroidered at selvedges.) Length of individual chain st is 4 k rows (see drawing). Keep embroidery tension loose so as not to "draw up" knitting.

Decrease for Top of Cap:
Row 1: K 2 tog across row, 40 sts remain.
Row 2: P.
Row 3: K 2 tog across row. Draw yarn through remaining 20 sts, pull tight and fasten. Seam selvedges together. Work another vertical row of chain sts over right side of seam. This is center back of cap. You will now have 8 vertical rows of chain sts spaced evenly around cap.

TASSEL

With contrasting yarn and crochet hook, sl st end of yarn to top of cap. *Ch 15, sl st to top of cap. Rep from * five times more. Break off yarn and weave in end.

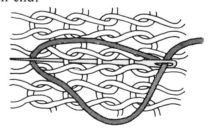

Safety Gift

By Evelyn Tuller, Elwood, Kansas

IF YOU have selected a high chair as a baby shower gift, give it an added touch of prettiness.

Buy a package of flower-shaped bathtub safety appliques and attach them to the seat of the high chair, then add some on the tray. They will keep the baby from sliding down in the chair when just learning to sit alone, and will keep the baby entertained.

Baby Wading Pool

By Evelyn Tuller, Elwood, Kansas

LOOKING FOR a different gift for a baby shower? How about an inflatable wading pool?

Include a baby blanket to be used in the bottom of the pool. When baby begins to crawl and turn over, the edges will serve as a soft play space, and will soften the blow in case of a fall. The pool is waterproof in case of an "accident", and it is a comfortable bed when nap time comes.

Baby Cradle Toy

So cute and fun to make, too!

By Mrs. Omar Stoutner, Keota, Iowa

Materials:
plastic "fashionese" needlepoint canvas
   (available in squares and hexagons at
   craft stores)
yarn
plastic lid from 2-pound coffee can
4 paper fasteners
flannel scraps
fiberfill
baby doll to fit

CUT THE fashionese to fit the length of a very tiny baby doll, and cut sides and a hood for the cradle to match. Work yarn ends in neatly as you needlepoint so the inside looks as smooth as the outside. Sew all pieces together, as shown. Cut the coffee can lid to resemble rockers, and attach at front and back of cradle with paper fasteners.

Make a little pad and blanket and put the doll in the cradle.

Baby Afghan

By Mrs. John Haag, Pipestone, Minnesota

Materials:
1 white, 40 x 81-inch rayon curtain panel (see
   photo at upper right)
2 skeins blue, 4-ply orlon acrylic yarn (or pink)
1 skein white, 4-ply orlon acrylic yarn
tapestry needle

TAKE THE hem out of the curtain, fold it crosswise and cut in half. Turn back each raw edge just enough to match one row of "holes" over another row of "holes". Baste.

Place the curtain on the table, and weave the blue yarn through the first row of holes ("A" row), over and under, as shown. Weave a second strand of blue yarn through the same row, next to the first strand.

In the next row ("B" row), weave white yarn over and under, using the smaller holes shown, until you reach the opposite side. With both colors, be sure to leave enough yarn free at each side, as shown, to make a knotted fringe.

Repeat each odd row with the two strands of blue, and the even rows, with one strand of white. Fringe. You still have another panel left to make another afghan!

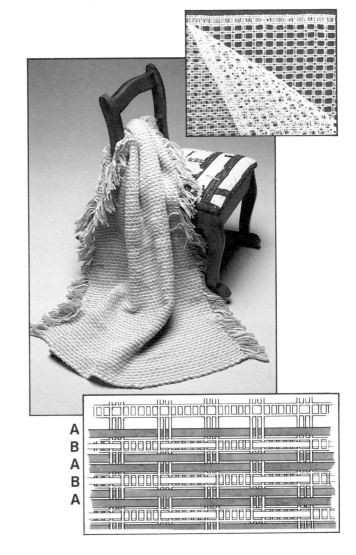

A
B
A
B
A
B
A

Diaper Cake

Are you looking for a pretty way to gift wrap some of those essentials?

By Mrs. Abe J. Miller, Fredericksburg, Ohio

Materials:
1 dozen gauze diapers
2 receiving blankets
1 sleeper
baby shawl
2 or 3 cards of diaper pins
3 strings of beads
1 pair baby booties
1 drinking cup
tiny rattles
small safety pins for pinning on scalloped
    beads

THIS FANCY cake is trimmed with all kinds of handy baby items Mom will be able to put to good use. And it's lovely to look at!

Each tier or layer is approximately 3 inches high. To get this dimension, first fold a diaper in half lengthwise, then fold in thirds, lengthwise.

To form the bottom layer of the cake, place the receiving blanket and sleeper in the center and wrap diapers around. It should take about six diapers to form the bottom layer.

Form the next layer by placing the baby shawl or other gift that's a bit bulky in the center, and wrap four diapers around. The top layer is formed by wrapping the remaining two diapers around the baby's drinking cup (turn the spout side down so the top is flat.)

Top off the cake by trimming it with a crocheted cap or baby booties. Other finishing touches include using pink or blue bows with tiny safety pins to hold rattles in place. Use diaper pins to pin the cake layers together and to join the ends where the diapers meet.

Bootie Pincushion

By Roylinda Rumbaugh, Mattawan, Michigan

Materials:
1/4-yard white felt
fiberfill
embroidery floss or crewel yarn
1/8-yard gingham or other print fabric
fabric glue
white thread
ribbon

CUT ONE of each pattern piece (see page 99). Match letters A, stitching by hand or with a 1/4-inch machine seam. Gather from point B to B (going through point C) on main piece. Match B's on the flap to B's on bootie main piece. Stitch, using 1/4-inch seam.

Embroider around bootie using a blanket stitch. Add a bow to the flap. Stuff. Cover with desired fabric, tucking in edges. Glue. Insert diaper pins.

Itty-Bitty Sandals

An adorable shower gift to make!

By Mrs. David Joens, Hopkins, Minnesota

(See crochet abbreviations on page 2.)

Size: Birth to 3 months. (Sole measures 3½ inches.)

Yarn: 1 ounce 4-ply lightweight orlon sayelle; small amount contrasting embroidery floss.

Crochet Hook: Size 5 or size that will give you correct gauge.

Gauge: 9 double crochet per inch.

SOLE

STARTING at center, ch 22 to measure 2½ ins.

Rnd 1: (Right side) Work 7 dc in 4th ch from hook, dc in next 17 ch, work 8 dc in last ch; working along opposite edge of starting ch, work dc in next 17 ch, join with sl st in 3rd ch of starting ch.

Rnd 2: Ch 3, dc in same place as sl st, work 2 dc in next 7 sts, dc in next 3 sts, hdc in next st, sc in next 2 sts, hdc in next st, dc in next 3 sts, tr in next 6 sts, 2 tr in each of next 10 sts (toe), tr in next 6 sts, dc in next 3 sts, hdc in next st, sc in next 2 sts, hdc in next st, dc in next 3 sts, join. Completed sole should measure 3½ ins.

HEEL

Row 1: With right side facing you, attach thread in back lp of next-to-last sc worked on last rnd; ch 3, dc in back lp of next 27 sts; ch 3, turn.

Row 2: Sk first dc, dc in each dc of last row and in turning ch; ch 3, turn.

Row 3: Rep last row.

Row 4: Sk first dc, dc in next dc, (ch 1, sk next dc, dc in next dc) 13 times (14 spaces around heel). Turn.

Row 5: Ch 3, sl st in 3rd ch from hook (picot made), sc in 1st sp, *make picot, sc in next sp. Rep from * 12 times more; picot, sc in same sp (15 picots). Break off.

STRAPS FOR INSTEP

Row 1: With right side facing you and counting from heel, sk 2 sts of sole, attach thread in back lp of next st, ch 2, dc in back lp of each of next 7 sts; ch 2, turn.

Row 2: Sk first dc, dc in next 7 sts; ch 2, turn. Rep last row 10 times more. Break off leaving a 12-in end for sewing. Make another strap on other side of sole in same manner. Cross straps over instep and sew ends to edge of sole.

TIES

Ch 4, sl st in 4th ch from hook, rep 4 more times to make rosette. Ch 100 and rep rosette. Break off and thread through spaces of heel. Decorate straps with embroidery as shown.

Lace Handkerchief

By Evelyn Tuller, Elwood, Kansas

A PRETTY finishing touch for your baby gift for a girl is a pretty lace handkerchief with an added notation "Something old for your wedding" written on the gift card, or embroidered on the handkerchief.

Signature Flannel Blanket

By Marla Fattig, Brady, Nebraska

SPREAD A baby blanket size piece of flannel on a card table, and as your guests arrive, ask them to "boldly" sign their name. Later, embroider the signatures, and fill in the center with the new baby's name, birth date, weight, etc. Make the flannel into a blanket for the new parents.

What Makes a Happy Child?

Mary Lamb Becker, a Milwaukee free-lance writer, talked to an adoption agency official about the factors parents should consider before having or adopting a child. From the interview, we see it takes more than time, energy and love...

By Mary Lamb Becker

IT WAS A pleasant lunch. As we ate, the conversation turned to the work my friend had recently retired from—placement for an adoption agency. Afterward, I thought about how she had described the thoroughness of her investigations and how she had been trained to seek out suitable adoptive families—those that would surely supply the best emotional, physical and moral climate in which a child could thrive and develop into the person God intended it to be.

I wondered if it might not be a good idea for natural parents-to-be to evaluate their own capabilities to rear a happy child.

What specific characteristics make successful parents? First of all, as parents we know ourselves. We are comfortable with ourselves and confident about who we are and what we have accomplished.

This may not be something an individual is consciously aware of. We might have to try to remember what it was like being a child ourselves. Who was the dominant person in our family—mother or father? How has our own upbringing affected our relationship with our spouse? How well do we understand each other? Do we know each other's shortcomings and strengths? How do our personalities dovetail?

How Do We Settle Problems?

How do we settle problems? Can we talk things out and avoid angry scenes?

Without allowing one's past to be an intimidating and limiting factor, our awareness of our past can help us face our day to day problems and help us solve them with insight and understanding.

Have we formed and do we keep up interpersonal relationships? Do we keep in touch with friends, close relatives? Do we have an extended family?

Do we have interests in the arts—music, dance, art and drama? Do we enjoy outdoor life and sports? Or, do we have tunnel vision in only one area? Will we provide opportunities for our child as best we can even if his talents lie in areas in which we personally have no interest?

How much self discipline have we shown as a couple? Have we kept a reasonably clean and orderly home? Are we spiritually self-disciplined? Are our beliefs backed up with actions? Is there a visible response and commitment to our moral and ethical beliefs? Do we attend church regularly?

Do We Want Too Much?

Are we financially self-disciplined? Can we keep our buying habits under control, or are we carried away with our wants—a new home, new car, clothes and vacations—without a realistic view of how these financial demands will be met if our situation changes?

Are we relying on two incomes now, unprepared for the restrictions that will have to made when a second income is sacrificed in order to care for an infant?

Will we be aware of the opportunities to stimulate our child's physical, mental and moral growth? Will we take time to read to him when he's young, to play games, to listen, to teach him the alphabet, to sing? All of these opportunities can slip by unnoticed and unattended to unless we recognize their importance.

One of the most frequent apprehensions of prospective parents is the possibility of having a handicapped child. What would our response be to that situation?

How patient will we be as parents? Will we give our child time to grow and to learn to love? Will we be ready to grow, understand and learn to love along with our children, recognizing that no matter the age, we are all persons becoming someone and not perfect finished models?

To a First-Time Mother

By Helen Rittell

Relax, my dear. Your little elf
Is just an amateur himself.
So if your hands, so newly filled
With tasks, seem somewhat less than skilled,
Relax, I say. This little pinkling
Doesn't have the slightest inkling
That you are new to baby lore—
He never had a Mom before!

— *Submitted by Mrs. David Joens,
Hopkins, Minnesota*

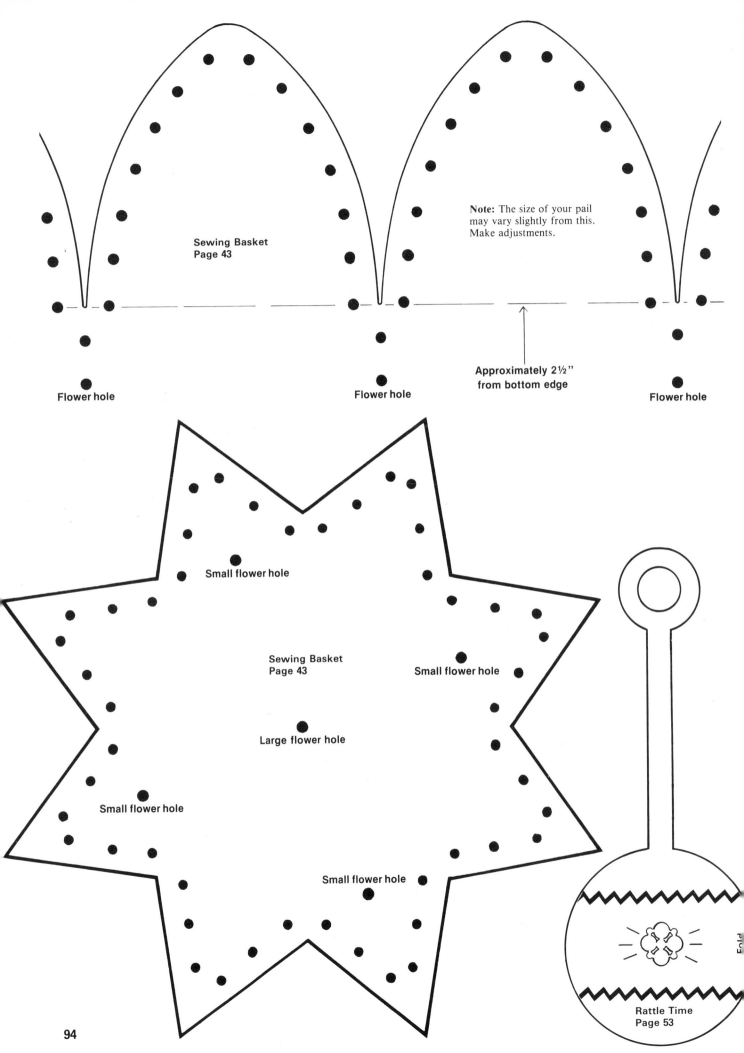

Sewing Basket
Page 43

Note: The size of your pail may vary slightly from this. Make adjustments.

Flower hole

Flower hole

Flower hole

Approximately 2½"
from bottom edge

Small flower hole

Sewing Basket
Page 43

Small flower hole

Large flower hole

Small flower hole

Small flower hole

Rattle Time
Page 53

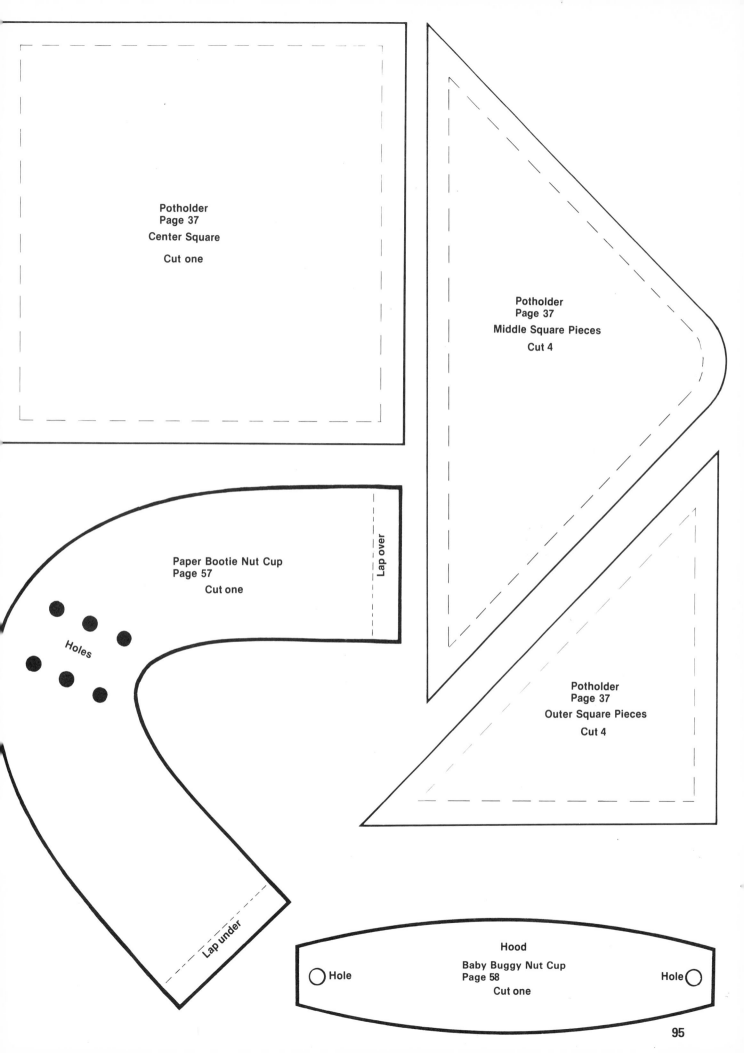

Potholder
Page 37
Center Square

Cut one

Potholder
Page 37
Middle Square Pieces
Cut 4

Lap over

Paper Bootie Nut Cup
Page 57
Cut one

Holes

Potholder
Page 37
Outer Square Pieces

Cut 4

Lap under

Hood

Baby Buggy Nut Cup
Page 58

Cut one

Hole

Hole

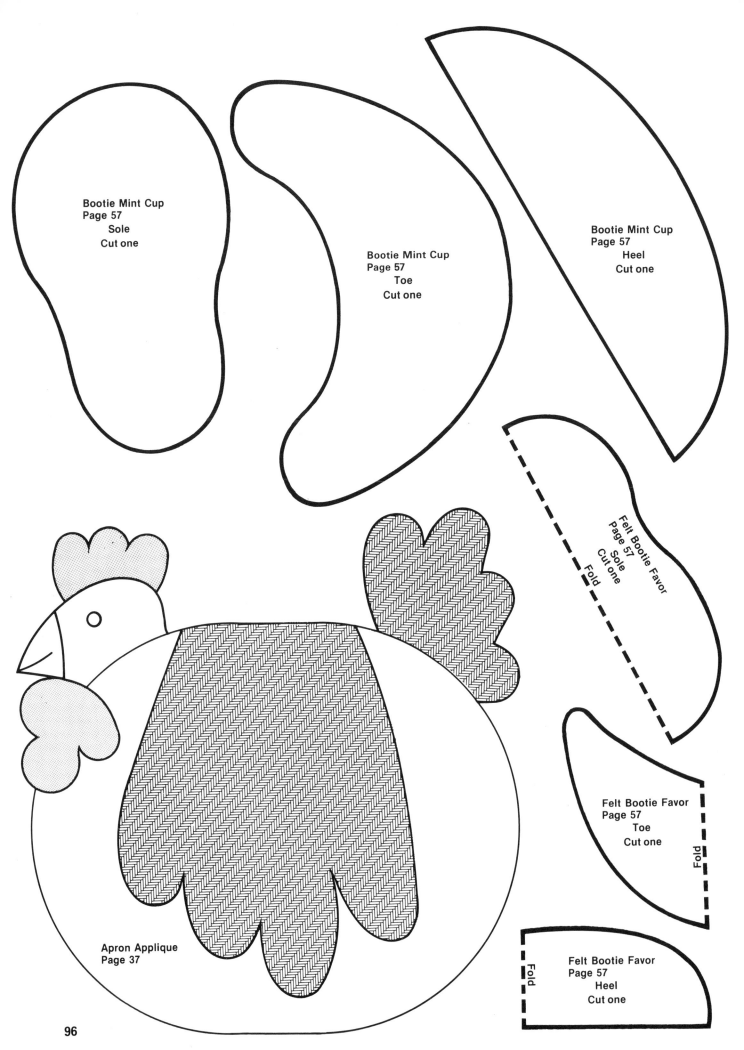

Bootie Mint Cup
Page 57
Sole
Cut one

Bootie Mint Cup
Page 57
Toe
Cut one

Bootie Mint Cup
Page 57
Heel
Cut one

Felt Bootie Favor
Page 57
Sole
Cut one
Fold

Felt Bootie Favor
Page 57
Toe
Cut one

Fold

Felt Bootie Favor
Page 57
Heel
Cut one

Fold

Apron Applique
Page 37

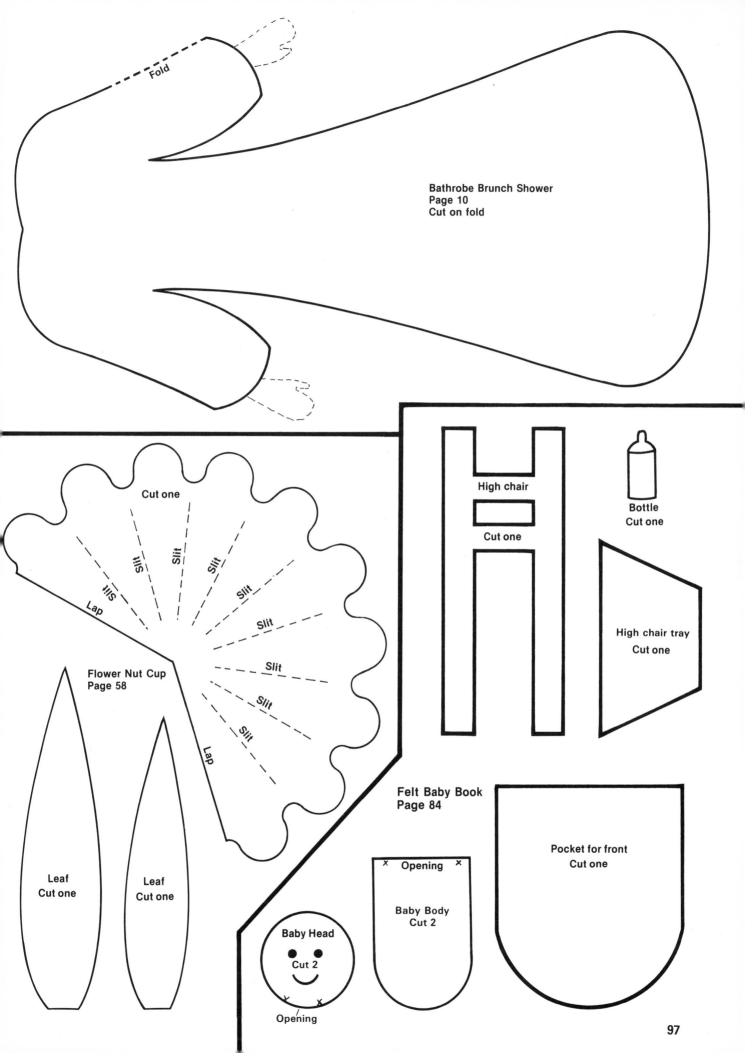

Fold

Bathrobe Brunch Shower
Page 10
Cut on fold

Cut one

Slit
Slit
Slit
Slit
Slit
Slit
Slit
Slit
Slit

Lap

Lap

Flower Nut Cup
Page 58

Leaf
Cut one

Leaf
Cut one

High chair

Cut one

Bottle
Cut one

High chair tray
Cut one

Felt Baby Book
Page 84

Pocket for front
Cut one

x Opening x

Baby Body
Cut 2

Baby Head
Cut 2

Opening

97

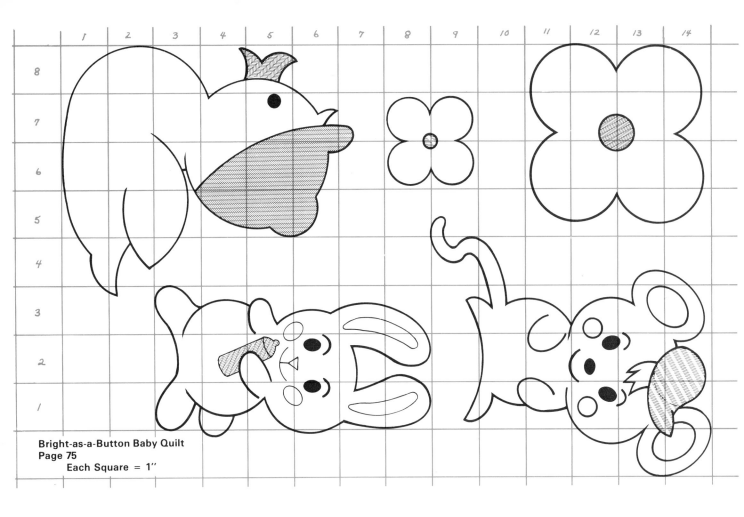

Bright-as-a-Button Baby Quilt
Page 75
Each Square = 1"

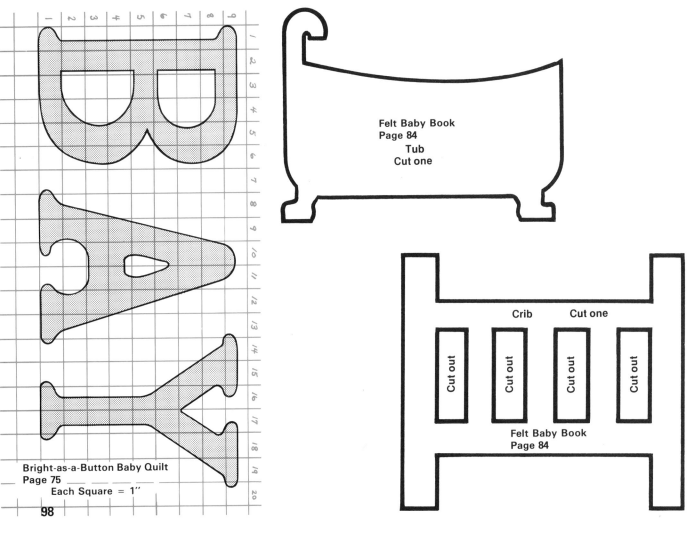

Felt Baby Book
Page 84
Tub
Cut one

Crib   Cut one

Cut out   Cut out   Cut out   Cut out

Felt Baby Book
Page 84

Bright-as-a-Button Baby Quilt
Page 75
Each Square = 1"

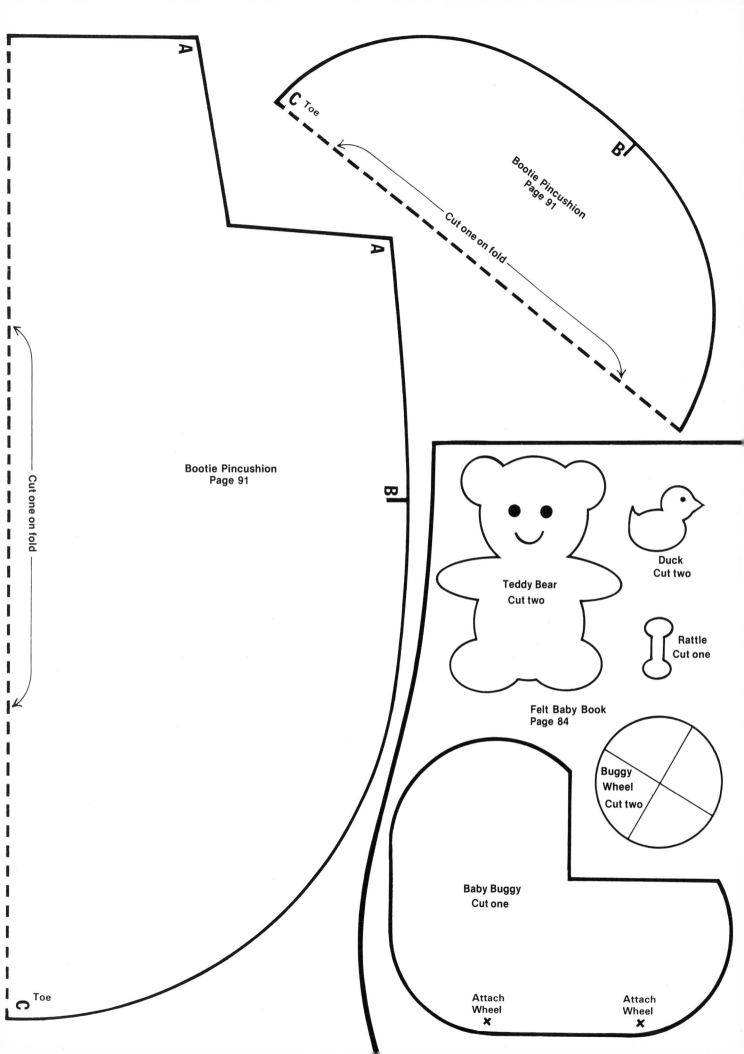

A

C Toe

B

Cut one on fold

Bootie Pincushion
Page 91

A

Bootie Pincushion
Page 91

Cut one on fold

B

Teddy Bear
Cut two

Duck
Cut two

Rattle
Cut one

Felt Baby Book
Page 84

Buggy
Wheel
Cut two

Baby Buggy
Cut one

Toe
C

Attach
Wheel
✗

Attach
Wheel
✗

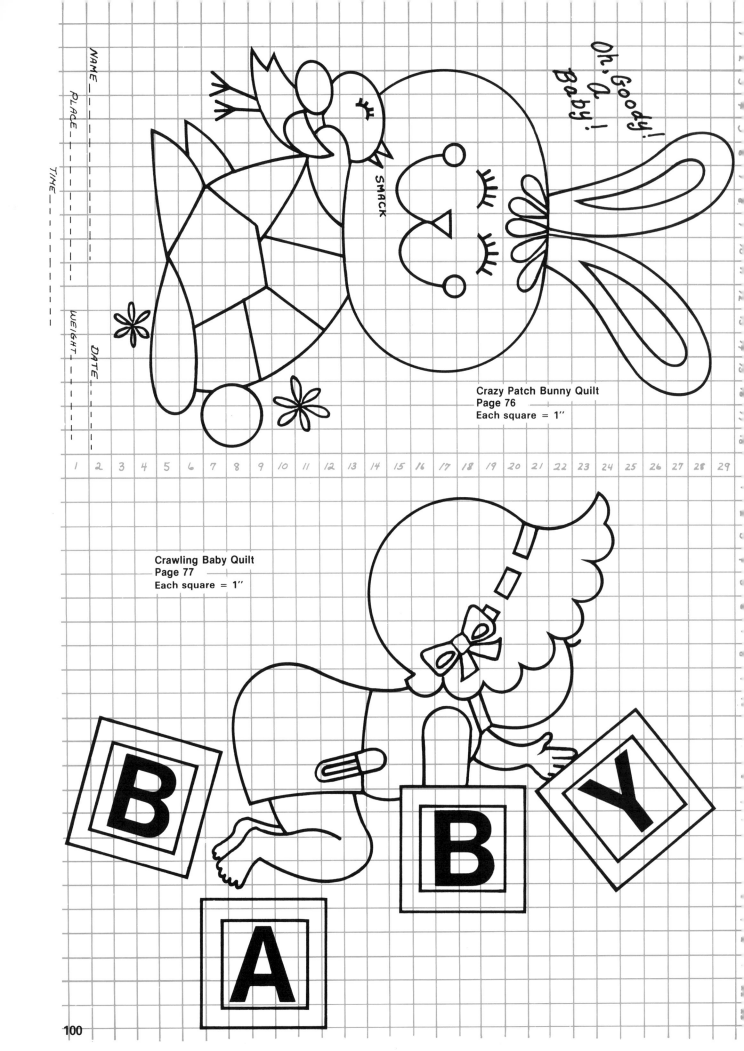

Crazy Patch Bunny Quilt
Page 76
Each square = 1″

Crawling Baby Quilt
Page 77
Each square = 1″

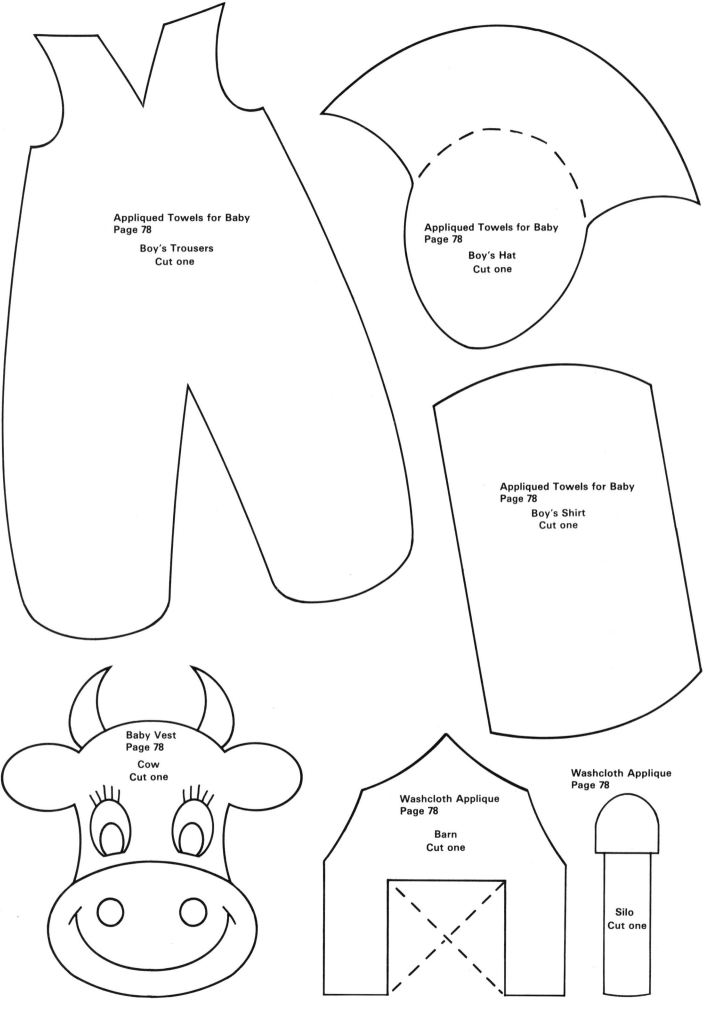

Appliqued Towels for Baby
Page 78

Boy's Trousers
Cut one

Appliqued Towels for Baby
Page 78

Boy's Hat
Cut one

Appliqued Towels for Baby
Page 78

Boy's Shirt
Cut one

Baby Vest
Page 78

Cow
Cut one

Washcloth Applique
Page 78

Barn
Cut one

Washcloth Applique
Page 78

Silo
Cut one

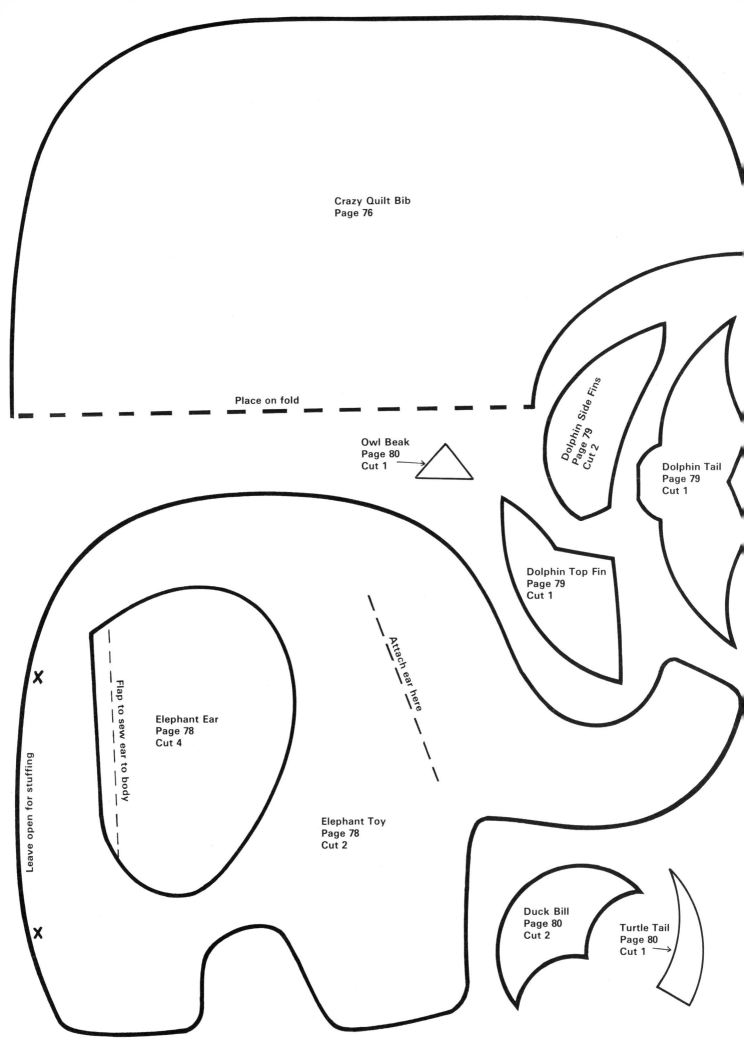

Crazy Quilt Bib
Page 76

Place on fold

Owl Beak
Page 80
Cut 1

Dolphin Side Fins
Page 79
Cut 2

Dolphin Tail
Page 79
Cut 1

Dolphin Top Fin
Page 79
Cut 1

Attach ear here

Flap to sew ear to body

Elephant Ear
Page 78
Cut 4

Elephant Toy
Page 78
Cut 2

Leave open for stuffing

Duck Bill
Page 80
Cut 2

Turtle Tail
Page 80
Cut 1

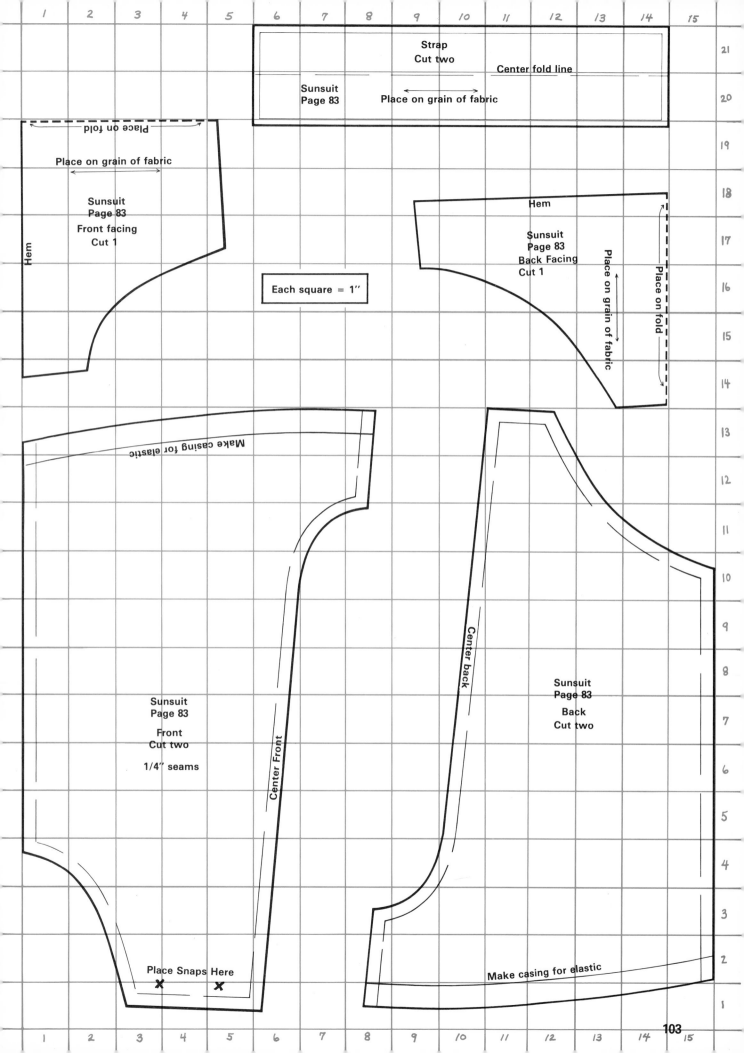

Strap
Cut two

Center fold line

Sunsuit
Page 83

Place on grain of fabric

Place on fold

Place on grain of fabric

Sunsuit
Page 83
Front facing
Cut 1

Hem

Each square = 1"

Hem

Sunsuit
Page 83
Back Facing
Cut 1

Place on grain of fabric

Place on fold

Make casing for elastic

Center Front

Center back

Sunsuit
Page 83

Front
Cut two

1/4" seams

Sunsuit
Page 83

Back
Cut two

Place Snaps Here

✗   ✗

Make casing for elastic

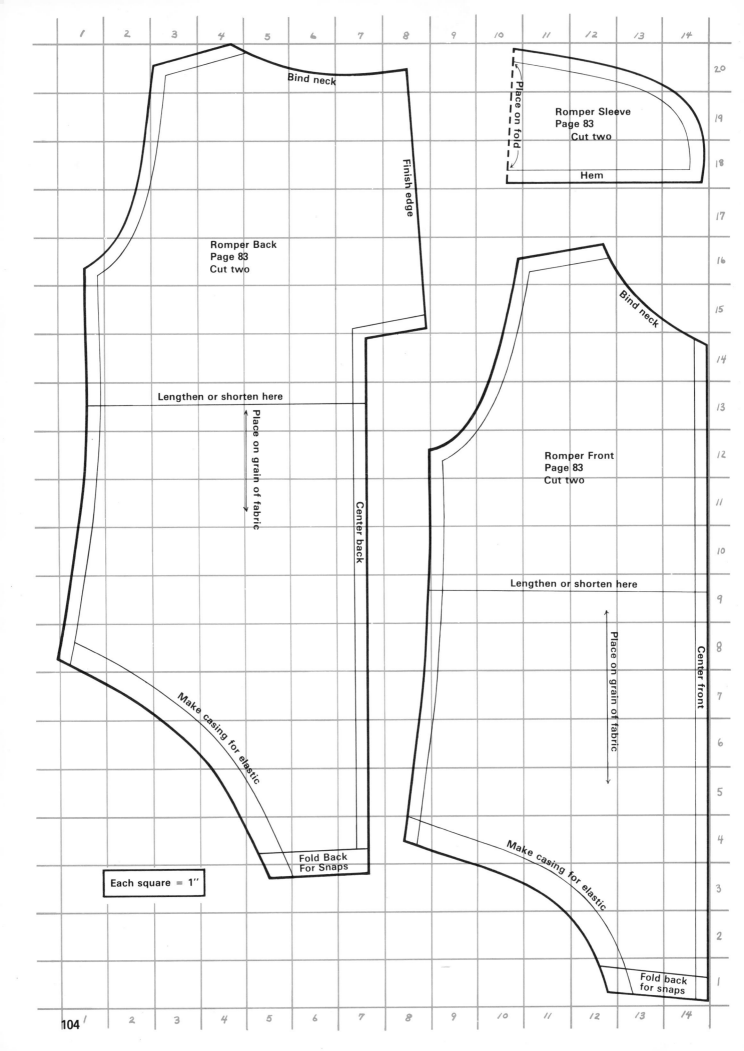

Bind neck

Finish edge

Romper Back
Page 83
Cut two

Place on fold

Romper Sleeve
Page 83
Cut two

Hem

Lengthen or shorten here

Place on grain of fabric

Center back

Make casing for elastic

Fold Back
For Snaps

Each square = 1″

Bind neck

Romper Front
Page 83
Cut two

Lengthen or shorten here

Place on grain of fabric

Center front

Make casing for elastic

Fold back
for snaps